OUTGROW MIDDLE MANAGEMENT

"Dave is a man of character and indomitable strength. His aura of wisdom commands respect among his peers and his influence creates relevant results. Dave shares his secrets to personal and professional success. If you want to rise above corporate limbo and bask in the happiness of actually living your life and career passions, read this book!"

—**Joseph Bismark**, Group Managing Director, Qi Group

"Dave is the perfect person to write this book as his career success is a testimonial to what drive, passion and dedication can do to ignite a career and launch it to the stratosphere. There is no better advice for aspiring young executives trying to climb the corporate ladder who feel stagnated, plateaued and stuck in middle management. It delivers!"

—**Patti Wilson**, The Career Company Founder

"Dave has authored a great book to help middle managers help their people and advance their careers at the same time. If you want to make a difference at work and propel your career at the same time, this is a must read book."

—**Michael Podolinsky**, Asia's Productivity Guru

OUTGROW MIDDLE MANAGEMENT

ACCELERATE YOUR CLIMB TO THE TOP

DAVE OSH

NEW YORK

OUTGROW MIDDLE MANAGEMENT
ACCELERATE YOUR CLIMB TO THE TOP

Published in New York, New York, by Morgan James Publishing. Morgan James and The Entrepreneurial Publisher are trademarks of Morgan James, LLC. www.MorganJamesPublishing.com

The Morgan James Speakers Group can bring authors to your live event. For more information or to book an event visit The Morgan James Speakers Group at www.TheMorganJamesSpeakersGroup.com.

A FREE eBook edition is available
with the purchase of this print book

CLEARLY PRINT YOUR NAME IN THE BOX ABOVE

Instructions to claim your free eBook edition:
1. Download the BitLit app for Android or iOS
2. Write your name in UPPER CASE in the box
3. Use the BitLit app to submit a photo
4. Download your eBook to any device

ISBN 978-1-63047-258-0 paperback
ISBN 978-1-63047-259-7 eBook
ISBN 978-1-63047-260-3 hardcover
Library of Congress Control Number:
2014931457

Cover Design by:
Rachel Lopez
www.r2cdesign.com

Interior Design by:
Bonnie Bushman
bonnie@caboodlegraphics.com

In an effort to support local communities, raise awareness and funds, Morgan James Publishing donates a percentage of all book sales for the life of each book to Habitat for Humanity Peninsula and Greater Williamsburg.

Get involved today, visit
www.MorganJamesBuilds.com

Habitat
for Humanity®
Peninsula and
Greater Williamsburg
Building Partner

DEDICATION

Dedicated to my incredible wife Ainsley, who encouraged me to write about my career ventures and become authentic publicly as much I was privately.

TABLE OF CONTENTS

MIDDLE MANAGEMENT HELL

ARE YOU STUCK IN MIDDLE MANAGEMENT HELL?

If this headline from Fortune magazine catches your eye, then this book is for you. Whether or not you agree that middle management is such a torture, life is indeed hard For America's 10.5 million middle managers, according to the Business Insider from August 7, 2013. The Wall Street Journal claimed that middle managers are being pushed to do more with less in their article, "What It's Like Being a Middle Manager Today." A recent Forbes magazine article had this threatening title: The End Of Middle Managers (And Why They'll Never Be Missed).

What's going on? Are middle managers at risk of going the way of the dinosaurs and facing extinction? Are **you** at risk? Is life for a middle manager going to be even more miserable than it currently is?

I have interviewed hundreds of middle managers over the last 20 years of my corporate career. In more than 25 different countries, I have begun to notice a substantial paradigm shift in the new challenges facing middle managers today. While in the last decade of the 20th century managers had consistent, sustainable

1

and enduring careers even in down markets, the wheel turned around at the beginning of the 21st century.

The majority of the candidates today hold positions 1.5 to 3 years, before hopping to another job. Corporate leaders excuse trend on a variety of factors: as a result of competitive talent market or shrugging their shoulders in surrender to the new economy. Generation gurus explain the trend as the new characteristics of generations X, Y, and Z. The reality is that there are new challenges beyond generation types. These challenges move and shake the lives of middle managers. The bad news is that neither middle managers, nor their bosses, know how to solve these problems.

What are the current challenges of middle managers that *Forbes* and *The Wall Street Journal* find so alarming? Are 10.5 Million Americans and an estimated 140 million middle managers around the world in serious problem?

Here are the top ten problems that appear consistently in various publications and employee surveys. Are any of these familiar to you? Are you facing one of them, a few of them or all of them?

1. STRESS, STRESS AND MORE STRESS

Middle managers are under the most stress in corporations because they face conflict from above and below. They are pushed by senior management above, whose decisions they are obliged to follow and below, by employees who must abide by the decisions without much explanation.

A study done by the Universities of Manchester and Liverpool has found that people in the middle hierarchy suffer the most social stress. The researchers say that highest level of stress hormones were recorded in middle groups who usually faced conflicts in their social and work lives.

Middle managers don't earn much more than junior employees. Their income is ridiculously low compared to senior executives who may earn even 10 times that of a middle manager. Stress because of financial matters causes relationship challenges, behavioral problems and health complications that could end with premature death.

As a result of unclear reporting lines, middle managers participate in many project teams without anyone at the top prioritizing their assignments. Unclear jobs requirements and success criteria increase the level of uncertainty, further increasing frustrations and stress. Turf wars between senior managers surge stress level in the people below who are expected to collaborate across department despite sometimes conflicting messages.

2. LACK OF CONTROL

Middle managers often assume more and more duties with too little authority. Many middle managers lack minimum autonomy. People without control and autonomy feel like they are in a cage—they are disengaged and discharged.

Out of control schedules are filled with meetings or consumed by sudden emergencies that only intensify an out of control sensation about career and life in general.

Middle managers are expected to execute whatever senior management comes up with but are rarely synched to the prime focus of the company. New directions may be completely misaligned with strategies that were just announced recently.

This combination of a lack of authority, autonomy and influence serves to widen the gap between upper management and middle management. It deepens the mistrust and increases confusion concerning what is the right thing to do. Periodic changes of plans outside the scope of the communicated strategy are common, especially when upper managers respond hysterically to events without engaging middle managers to resolve new challenges.

3. GAPS BETWEEN CAREER AND PERSONAL ASPIRATIONS

Many middle managers, when asked about their own personal aspirations, shared with me that their ambitions were completely unrelated to their career paths. Many said that their dream was to be his or her own boss. It is no wonder that get rich schemes use the popular tagline, "Fire your boss!" It touches on the untapped dreams of most middle managers. The wider the gap between career and personal aspirations, the more frustrated people become.

4. CAREER PLATEAU

There can be many causes for a career to plateau, but there is one obvious result. You are stuck in your position without moving upward. Many professionals who have been promoted rapidly from non-management to middle management, discover that their initial fast momentum comes to an abrupt halt in middle management.

When you are stuck, everything looks gloomy. You start thinking that you're in the wrong profession. You dislike your boss or you feel like you don't fit the corporate culture. It's similar to a car breaking down in the middle of nowhere, in the middle of the night. Just like a car stopping all at once, the same can happen with your career. Once you stall, it can take years to develop new momentum. The longer it takes, the lower the chances to break through. It takes even longer to recover career downturns as a result of terminations, layoffs or self-initiated breaks for maternity leave or a pursuit of higher education, such as a Master's degree.

I have met many middle managers who began as mavericks and suddenly stalled long before they reached their full potential. Their common mistake was focusing the blame on their employers, instead of taking corrective actions.

Career advancement and promotions become more and more difficult to achieve. Companies have cut out so many management levels, that the leap to the next level is often a greater distance and is therefore, harder to accomplish. As a result you get fancier titles for just doing the same job without a substantial upgrade.

In a flat, or level organization, there is less potential for promotions—there is no hierarchy to scale the corporate pinnacle. Organizations have become a maze of team leaders, project leaders and many undefined titles that are a reflection of the disruptive change in organizational structures.

Middle managers are stuck also because of the "Gray Ceiling." Upper management doesn't seem to retire as young as they used to. The entitlement age for Social Security heads north while employer retirement benefits head south. As a result, baby boomers cannot afford to retire because they don't have enough savings.

5. FINANCIAL CONSTRAINTS

The average annual income of middle managers is around $50,000. This income might be sufficient for singles, but married couples with children usually struggle financially because of the burdens of mortgage payments, education costs, living expenses and inflating credit card debts.

It seems that the rewards never match the investment in education. Having a Bachelor degree or a Master's degree doesn't necessarily yield in higher returns. Middle managers feel under-compensated. They see less educated and less capable employees earning more, while doing jobs that require less competence.

6. FEAR OF LAYOFFS

In this turbulent economic world, market shifts can change positions of companies very rapidly. A company that owns its market can lose it very quickly to a new competitor. Overnight, the competition that introduces disruptive technology can win the market share, while your employer loses customers.

Unfortunately most companies respond to disruptive competition with layoffs instead of counter innovation. As a result, top talent quits and the rest live in fear of the next lay-off wave.

In this situation no one wants to innovate because no one wants to risk failure. The remaining managers face higher workload and less investment in training and development because their employers cut costs.

7. WORK OVERLOAD

Middle managers complain that year after year their workdays become longer while their lunch breaks become shorter. Their weeks become longer while their vacations become shorter. Many middle managers complain that they don't have time to go out for lunch. They eat at their desk because they fear that they cannot complete their to-do-list if they take time off for a lunch break. Workload grows as companies become lean, mean and flat with as few management layers as possible.

Laptops, smartphones and mobile applications extend the working days to late nights and endless weekends. Colleagues send messages at 9pm and expect immediate response because everybody is connected. If you don't respond quickly, you became irrelevant. So the solution is to hold your smartphone on the dinner table and start typing maniacally every few minutes. As a result, you stop listening to your partner or your kids who are sharing their exciting stories of their day.

Middle managers used to have secretaries, assistants and administrative staff to help them with administrative work. No more. You have to do it all by yourself because all the tools are at your fingertips.

International corporations provide new challenges. When you finish your day in your company's headquarters in the United States, your customers and colleagues or direct reporting teams are just beginning their day in China, India, or South East Asia. While your spouse and children's lives are going on around you, you attend urgent conference calls. Then you have to summarize the calls around midnight to inform your boss of the action plans.

40-hour week jobs have evolved into 24 hours a day, 365 days a year. Nine-hour day employment contracts have informally become 15-hour days. As a junior staff member, you were entitled for overtime compensation. As a middle manager, you lose this benefit and in many cases actually earn less than your junior staff per hour.

8. OUTDATED COMPETENCIES

Middle managers face rapid shift of competencies. What they learned in college may have become obsolete by the time they graduated. Middle management positions that traditionally spend significant time monitoring, controlling and reporting have been replaced by integrated systems that do all these functions automatically. Business Intelligence technologies produce accurate, timely and interactive reports and may make middle managers redundant.

Even analysts who were proud of their craft and were once carefully listened to by senior management, have been bypassed by Big Data analytics that provide insights into every aspect of the business in real time. To save your job you either become faster than a super computer or alternatively gain new competencies that add more value to your business.

This trend doesn't appear to be slowing down. It accelerates and challenges jobs that we currently wouldn't even consider replacing. Can you imagine a physician who diagnoses you online, prescribes you a medicine online and has it delivered to your home in two hours?

Many professions will experience rapid disruptions and will require new competencies. You have to be prepared in order to stay on top of your game.

9. IMPERSONAL WORKPLACE

Our workplace was once the most common place to develop friendships. In years past, we've traditionally spent more time in the office or at the manufacturing site or customer sites, than our own home. We want to relate, communicate and develop relationships. While in the old economy, we worked with colleagues for many years; in the new economy, job-hopping is the new golden standard.

While face-to-face conversations were the way to confront, elaborate and brainstorm, emails and chat rooms have replaced these face-to-face methods of communication. People attend the same conference call sitting in their cubicles or offices instead of sharing a location. It is typical to see two people choose to exchange argumentative email instead of having coffee together to resolve the matter. The more digital the workplace becomes, the more impersonal it becomes.

10. DISTRACTING COMMUNICATION

Digital communication has opened vast opportunities to communicate economically, with virtually anyone in the world. Through audio, video or writing in real-time, we can cross continents in a matter of seconds using digital media tools.

The same tools that make our world so exciting also make our world less productive. It is difficult to concentrate. It is difficult to complete a simple task before a new notification appears on our screens, distracting us from the task at hand.

Digital distraction makes us less efficient because when you stop a task, it takes four times longer to continue from where you stopped than if you hadn't stopped. Digital distraction kills creativity. The more responsive you become, the less productive you become. The more you cater to digital interruptions, the less creative you are. This nonstop digital noise is an artificial overload. The ability to copy dozens of people on email exchange creates an information overload. Your email inbox is filled with hundreds of emails in just a few hours.

If you face any or all of the problems mentioned above, they represent an enormous impact on your career and your life. Unfortunately, it won't be getting any easier. You will continue to experience more turbulent shifts in the workplace, with bigger impact on your life.

The good news is that there is a solution. A new approach is needed to be successful in the new economy. The losers in the new world will be executives who will try hard to improve their efficiency, work harder, and just do better than what they have been doing so far. The winners will be executives who can adapt new career and life strategies that will enable them to stand out from the rest of the herd. All of this while adding significant value, scaling the corporate ladder, achieving financial freedom without stress, and feeling fulfilled, loved, happy, and healthy.

ADVERSITIES

Picture this: It's early on a weekend morning in the year 2000. I'm standing in front of a large picture window, a cup of coffee in my hand, with Hong Kong's Victoria Harbor stretched out before me. I live in the tallest residential tower in Asia Pacific, surrounded by spectacular views of the harbor, The Peak and a crystal blue sky filled with skyscrapers. I watch as a giant luxury cruise liner gracefully approaches Ocean Terminal. The iconic cross-harbor Star ferries silently give way to the enormous ship. I am on top of Hong Kong but I feel like I am on top of the world, on the top of my game, on the top of my career.

A trail of Rolls-Royces, Bentleys and Ferraris depart from the tower and descend along Old Peak Road. Drivers are stretched in front of the latest models of the most expensive cars in the world, waiting to drive residents to golf clubs around the island.

It feels like a dream, but this is my reality. This luxury $10,000 a month rented apartment is my home. I am the Vice President, Asia Pacific of a hi-tech company. My kids study in top-notch international schools. We travel the exotic

Far East for business and pleasure, employ a live-in maid and host lavish parties for our community.

My stock options value climbed above the million-dollar mark, only 18 months after receiving them from my employer. My private stock portfolio, managed by a prestigious brokerage firm, has reached 500,000 dollars. My net worth is almost 2 million. I am damn lucky!

I take a moment to think back to just five years ago. At the time, my 30,000 dollar annual income just barely covered my mortgage payments, car loan installments and over limit credit card debt, which I couldn't get rid of. My wife and I lived from one salary to the next, from bill to bill. We couldn't afford vacations other than the redemptions of credit card points. Our cost of living skyrocketed after the second child was born. Overdraft warning calls from the bank increased our stress, anxiety and feelings of helplessness.

It shouldn't have been that way. We were both professionals who graduated with Bachelors degrees in economics, who worked hard for MBA's and CPA certifications. But we couldn't pay our bills with credentials.

I quit the accounting firm to assume a Financial Controller position in a large paper mill company. The income increased to $50,000 per year but that didn't improve our financial constraints. Our expenses soon outpaced the new income while increased interest and inflation rates doubled our house loan liability over time.

My efforts to move to a higher paying industry or profession failed. Recruiters repeated the same old script: "Your education is finance, your experience is finance. It's too late to change career path when you're already in middle management."

The financial struggle drove me to develop a new career roadmap. I started a new business parallel to my day job, acquired new competencies, attended seminars, read sales and marketing books and studied English all in an attempt to be hired for an international assignment.

Two years later, I am in Hong Kong. I am an expatriate, or what we call an expat. I earn 10 times the income I earned only 5 years earlier. More importantly, I'm debt free.

I continue to look at the astounding view of the green mountainous jungles and the blue sea right outside my home. I turn away from the window with a great feeling of accomplishment. I don't spare a moment to debate whether my success tower is built on a solid rock or on shifting sand.

It doesn't take long to find out. In the beginning of 2000, the Internet Bubble bursts. In just a few months, my million-dollar paper wealth of stock options has evaporated into nothing. My company's sales plunge abruptly. Massive layoffs follow poor financial results. I call my broker to sell my portfolio and discover it is too late—we have lost half of our real savings. My wealth illusion ends brutally.

A few months later, my wife and I decide to divorce after a 15-year marriage. It is very painful to leave home and be far away from my children. Divorce is tough. Unexpected divorce is even tougher. The emotional turmoil of breaking up a family could fill another book! Going through this hell, we sell our house for a loss and I am left with only a fraction of my imaginary wealth from just few months earlier.

The combination of my company's plummeting performance and my deteriorating personal performance due to the divorce begins to take a toll. The result is that my contract is not renewed. My only chance to stay in Asia Pacific is to accept an offer for the wrong position in the wrong profession but in the right country - Singapore. I assume a CFO role for a large semiconductor company in Singapore however, after a few months the company merges with another company. I'm not the CFO of the merged company.

Fortunately I am granted a Permanent Resident status just before the merger. My career stalls and for the first time in my life, I am unemployed. Without any financial support for my children's international schools and without any other income, my savings drain rapidly. I start a new business but I know it'll take time to yield significant income. I'm back to square one. I struggle financially again. It is even worse than before. I am jobless and my career is stuck. The only good news is that the worst has already happened; I've hit rock bottom and the only direction is up. Or so I thought.

While applying for a Permanent Residence in Singapore, I am required to do a medical check. A few days after the medical check, a nervous voice calls me and asks me to come to see a specialist in the hospital.

The hematologist is looking at me calmly but choosing his words carefully: "Sir, your blood platelets count is 1.2 million while the normal range is 150,000 to 400,000 per microliter (mcL). You have a condition called Essential

Thrombocythemia (ET). It is a chronic form of leukemia where bone marrow makes too many platelets. You are at serious risk of blot clots which can lead to stroke, heart attack and even sudden death."

"What's the cure?" I ask.

"Unfortunately, there is no cure for this rare condition. The only treatment that has some success is chemotherapy medication," the hematologist explains.

"For how long?"

His answer hits me like a bullet.

"For life."

10 minutes later, I leave the hospital and my head is spinning. That's it? Is this the end? In one year I have lost my family, my job, my wealth, my health, and maybe even my life.

I ask myself: Have I lived fully? Have I mattered to people? Have I made any difference?

I hate my answers to these questions.

What I felt in front of the window with my view of the world in Hong Kong was a false success. It was not sustainable. It compromised every aspect of my life. I was so consumed by my career and financial success that I forgot to live. I neglected my loved ones. I had my priorities all wrong.

Not only was my success unreal; I also continuously wore a façade, masking how I really felt. I never shared my struggles with my friends. I was never vulnerable or asked for help. When someone would ask how I was doing, I faked a smile and lied about how great it all was, even when every aspect of my life was falling apart. It was more important for me to keep up the façade.

It was already midnight when my head suddenly stopped spinning. I began to feel a sense of relief and the heaviness in my chest faded quickly. I close my eyes and begin to envision a new life coming ahead. I start laughing—this is insane! I should feel defeated after hearing the news about my disease and the risk of death I'm facing, but instead I feel reborn to new life. This moment. Now.

I visualize starting a new business; leading a large organization and helping millions of people improve their lives. I visualize that I'm healthy, fit and energetic—in the best shape ever. I visualize that I love and am loved by family and friends. I reach success without side effects. I accomplish my goals while staying connected and fully present in my relationships.

I finally fall asleep at dawn.

A few years later, my vision has come true. I'm the CEO of an international business. I own an Internet enterprise that empowers people. I'm remarried to an amazing wife who shares my passions. I have a new daughter and we're deeply connected emotionally. I travel the world. I'm a role model of health and fitness with a platform to inspire thousands of people and help them improve their wellbeing. I earn more than my previous temporary peak, but more importantly, I live a balanced life. My family's net worth is in the millions of dollars. Our children study at top universities and international schools. I find time for family vacations, safari trips, skiing, and windsurfing. I replace my ego driven management style with service and coaching leadership. I love. I dare. I care. I share. I begin to write. I begin speaking publicly. I live fully.

The one thing I haven't done until this moment is to share my true story about my incurable disease. The first time I told my story to a friend, her eyes opened wide in surprise. "This is an incredible story, Dave. Everybody is jealous of your super fitness and health. Your story becomes even more inspirational when we know you suffer an incurable disease. Go tell your story, buddy."

So I did.

I want you to know that there is a way to overcome challenges in your life. There is way to live fully while having a great career, earning an incredible living and making a difference for you, your loved ones, friends, colleagues and the community. The solution is to bring together all aspects of your life and align them together toward one direction. If I can do this, you can too.

BLUEPRINT FOR SUCCESS

Most of the executives I have interviewed throughout my career are middle managers. I continued to interview candidates for middle management positions even after becoming a CEO of a multinational corporation. My team didn't like it. They thought that I shouldn't be bothered interviewing logistics managers, applications managers or customer service managers.

They had many reasons they didn't want the CEO to interview their preferred candidates. First, I was known for being a tough interviewer. Second, they didn't want to hire middle managers that hadn't passed the CEO's interview.

The truth is that I interviewed for completely different reasons and for different positions than the hiring managers believed. I interviewed to find out whether the candidates had the potential to replace the hiring managers in the future. I interviewed to find out if the hiring managers had the guts to hire somebody better than him or herself. I interviewed to find out whether the candidates had potential to replace the managers of the hiring managers, or ultimately even myself, in the future.

Sadly, the candidates were not ready for being interviewed for a higher level or the highest level in the corporate ladder. They were ready mentally, intellectually and emotionally for just being interviewed for... middle management. If they get the job, they act as middle managers and expect a few years later, with some additional education and experience, to be promoted to senior management. But what about when this doesn't happen?

You meet these people at the cafeteria or at the water fountain. They complain regularly about how badly they are being treated because there is no promotion for them on the horizon.

The truth is, if you want to quickly outgrow middle management into senior management and top management, you have to start behaving like a C-Suite executive now. The sooner you behave like a top executive, the faster you'll become one; the faster you'll multiply your income, control your time and achieve congruence in your life. It is a self-fulfilling prophecy.

I want to help these executives get it right faster and avoid the pitfalls I've gone through. It took me years to figure out the roadmap to accomplish a fulfilling, meaningful and rewarding corporate career that is fully integrated with my aspirations, ambitions and passions.

I started to blog my new strategies with an aim to improve the career and lives of the 500 employees in my company who spread across 25 countries. Surprisingly, other executives like you all around the world, have begun to follow my teachings.

After 3 years of publishing, speaking, coaching and mentoring, I noticed accelerated growth in my followers and even in myself. I identified six key strategies that enable executives to scale the corporate pinnacle much faster and with much better career-life harmony. People that have followed these strategies love their jobs and love their lives.

The accelerated journey of outgrowing middle management is through the development of two domains: Inner Leadership and Outer Leadership.

Inner Leadership is also known as Personal Leadership. It is your presence, abilities, beliefs, emotions and unconscious habits. At its heart is your self-awareness and growth toward self-mastery. It is your sense of connection with those around you. It's also the source of your outer leadership. Inner leadership is the enhancement of your presence and the cultivation of the right attitude toward other people.

Outer Leadership is the behavior that influences other people; whether individually in one-on-one conversations or as a group, simultaneously impacting a group of people during meetings, conference calls or presentations. Outer Leadership is the art of motivating individuals and groups with a shared purpose and vision. It is the way to build team spirit that ultimately leads to actions and progress toward results.

Inner Leadership is the foundation for successful Outer Leadership. Inner Leadership enables you to build trusting relationships with followers while staying connected to your core values. You have to lead yourself first before you lead others. Self-mastery of Inner Leadership will empower you to lead, regardless of your title or position and even without authority. It is crucial in today's flat and collaborative organizations.

Inner Leadership focuses on emotional intelligence, assertiveness, setting goals, developing character, gaining adaptive skills, creating abundant mindset and daring to challenge yourself and others. Inner Leadership allows you to let go of unconscious past limiting beliefs and restraining habits. It also enables you to connect more strongly with purpose and values so that your leadership presence authentically serves those you lead.

Once you master Inner Leadership you can take the next step toward Outer Leadership. The common mistake most corporate executives face is the challenge of one-on-one conversations or group discussions. They tend to focus on their group skills without being aware that the biggest challenge is inside rather than outside.

When it comes to Outer Leadership, consider that the groups you work with within an organization are comprised of individuals that vary in their ambition, confidence and experience. You know most of these individuals and you probably have relationships with some or most of them. The path to successful Outer Leadership starts with one-on-one conversations with individual members of the groups. Many of us avoid uncomfortable conversations, because we're afraid that they will affect work relationships. Avoidance of such encounters at the private level ends up ultimately affecting our ability to reach support, get resolution or conclude action plans when addressing bigger groups.

Inner Leadership and Outer Leadership help you to attain inner alignment of self-identity and purpose that will eventually lead to freedom from fear. Through the process, you will reveal your authentic self, letting your uniqueness flow and motivate others. It's your unique genuine presence that inspires people to trust you.

The three strategies that develop your Inner Leadership are Intention, Expansiveness and Effectiveness.

The three strategies that develop Outer Leadership are Dialogue, Decision and Action.

Let's master each of the six strategies successfully so that you will make a difference in your own career and life, and even more powerfully, in the careers and lives of the people you engage.

INNER LEADERSHIP

Intention

Intention means to perform any act or series of acts with specific purpose so that it leads to the outcomes you have in mind. On the surface, intentional behavior is to act deliberately upon goals. However, it is more than that. Intentional behavior: defines a desired purpose that achieves desired destination, sets core values that guide you on the best route, and develops the courage you need to overcome obstacles.

Surprisingly, most people focus on the mechanism rather than the intention. Thus, the outcomes are unintentional and not rewarding. Being intentional is the first step toward self-mastery. It will make the biggest impact on your character and behavior.

Expansiveness

Expansiveness is the ability to expand your world to areas beyond your expertise, education or comfort zone. The secret to succeeding in your career and life is to continue to grow and learn new skills. Expanding your world into new areas of expertise will open up new opportunities.

You want to grow beyond your current expertise to become a leader. You want to develop your right and left-brain to become creative. You want to enhance your strengths. You want to improve your emotional reactions to events. All of these are examples of expansive behavior. People identify with quickly expansive people. Expansive people constantly improve their characters and behaviors. They continuously grow their professional and personal knowledge. They are lifelong learners.

Effectiveness

Effectiveness is the capability to make an impact and to affect the end result of processes. Ultimately, being effective is the most important characteristic of senior executives. Effectiveness is required to move up from middle management to the top of the corporate ladder. While junior executives are evaluated positively for being productive and efficient, middle managers are evaluated for being effective, on top of being efficient and productive. Ultimately, effectiveness is what differentiates middle from senior management.

OUTER LEADERSHIP

Dialogue

Dialogues are the conversations you have with your peers. Conversations are the foundation of all the decisions and the actions that your team will execute. Conversations carry the seeds for any change that your customers, vendors, business partners or board members will adopt. Once you know that everything starts with intention, you realize the importance of being able to articulate your ideas in order to achieve your goals.

The most important skill for an effective dialogue is communication. It is what separates a great idea that is executed successfully from a great idea that fails to receive attention and gets lost in the noise and clutter.

If you want to leapfrog to the next level and beyond, communication is the single most important Outer Leadership skill that you can cultivate to get you there. Good communication is the ability to conduct honest, crucial one-on-one conversations with peers. It is the key to developing trust, confronting others when required, establishing commitment, and providing accountabilities in order to get results. It is imperative that you develop public speaking skills, be able to tell passionate stories, connect enthusiastically, stop Power Point addiction and influence through emotional, as well as logical, reasoning.

Decision

Decision-making is easier when the dialogue aspect is done correctly. Common challenges we often face are those conversations that are left hanging in mid-air, without conclusive decisions. You have probably attended meetings where everyone left with different opinions of what needed to get done because the decision-making was not done properly, if it was even done at all.

There must be clear definition between ending the dialogue and starting the decision-making process. Even when you jump between dialogue and decision-making, always distinguish between the two.

During the dialogue stage, it is important that all voices are heard, however, in the decision-making process you have to ensure you get commitments for the decision from all relevant people. At some point, everyone has to accept the position and support it, whether or not they advocated for it. This ability to "disagree and commit" was popularized by the CEO of Intel, Andy Grove.

Action

Action is the act of execution. As much as we all bring good intention to our work, appraisals and rewards are based on results rather than intentions. The only way to get results is to get things done. Great ideas, awesome presentations and gigantic investments have been known to evaporate into thin air because of lousy execution.

Poor execution is usually blamed as the reason for failures, but we tend to ignore that execution typically fails because the previous steps have not been successfully implemented. Perhaps the plans executed didn't receive full support from all the people that participated, thus they didn't contribute to the execution. Or the project team didn't fully understand the plan because they hadn't participated in the dialogue. It could be that the leader didn't verify commitment for the decision before the execution. Or that the dialogue was not open to all voices or people were not allowed to freely express objections or were afraid to speak openly because of corporate politics or culture.

Now that you have the six steps to success blueprint to Outgrow Middle Management, you shouldn't miss promotion opportunities. The biggest obstacle is an ignorance of Inner Leadership. Don't focus solely on Outer Leadership just because this is where problems appear externally. The roots of the problems are found within ourselves. Unless we master ourselves, we will never master others. This is today's corporate game. If you want to win this game, you have to learn how to play it

Following the flow of the blueprint will help you overcome this obstacle. First, become Intentional, Expansive and Effective. Then, master your endeavors through Dialogue Decision and Action.

PART I
INNER LEADERSHIP

INTENTION

TRANSFORM FROM MANAGER TO LEADER

There is a lot of confusion about the differences between management and leadership. They both involve deciding what needs to be done, creating a network of people to accomplish goals and ensuring that the work actually gets done. Management and leadership complement each other, but they do so in a very different way.

So what is the difference?

John P. Kotter differentiates management from leadership in his book, *What Leaders Really Do*. He claims that management copes with complexity but leadership copes with rapid change. Kotter has discovered three major differences between management and leadership:

1. Management involves setting goals, planning, budgeting and allocating resources. Leadership involves setting direction and developing a vision of the future, along with strategies to achieve this vision.

2. Management involves organizing, staffing, and setting-up job descriptions, recruiting qualified individuals, delegating responsibilities and devising systems to monitor execution. Leadership involves aligning people, communicating the vision and getting a commitment to achieve it.

3. Management provides control, solves problems, monitors results versus objectives and takes corrective actions to resolve deviations. Leadership provides motivation and inspiration. It keeps people moving in the right direction despite challenges, by appealing to their values and emotions.

Most organizations are over-managed and under-led because they focus mainly on formal long-term planning and budgeting rather than on setting a direction. Long-term planning is a deductive process, while setting direction is an inductive process. Long term planning worked well in the 20th century when the markets did not change rapidly. In the 21st century, markets are characterized by rapid change and we must adapt to volatile market dynamics. Therefore rapid change is essential to be able to compete in the new dynamic business environment.

But here is the problem…

Managers try forcing change through formal organizational systems, structures and incentives. They fail to drive change because they don't involve informal stakeholders (like customers or suppliers). Managers communicate short-term plans effectively through the formal organization, but when it comes to communicating a whole new future – you need a leader.

Communicating a new vision successfully depends solely on leadership – not management. Leaders tend to go beyond the mechanical structure of the organization. While managers count on the power of their titles, leaders count on rapport, integrity and trustworthiness to drive change.

Well-managed organizations are not necessarily well-led organizations. The employees of well-managed organizations are effective within the Standard Operating Procedures (SOP). The same employees are powerless when they try to initiate change outside the SOP. When they attempt to initiate change, they receive responses like, "That's against our policy" or "We cannot afford it" or "Shut-up and do as you are told."

Strong leaders resolve these challenges by providing a strong alignment and drive change beyond SOP. While managers focus on "best practices," leaders create "new practices." While managers adapt to the culture; leaders create a new culture. Leaders align employees with the new direction and ensure that they are not reprimanded, even when they do not comply with the policy.

For example, managing a factory requires an effective control system to respond immediately to deviations from the plan. This factory requires well organized, trained and disciplined employees to run the plant efficiently. But achieving a bold vision requires the kind of energy that only motivated, empowered and inspired employees can achieve. Control systems will not drive employees toward a new direction. Leaders, not managers, will evoke feelings of achievement, a sense of belonging, recognition, self-esteem, and a valuable purpose. Such feelings will prompt powerful responses.

Leaders, rather than managers, will motivate their people by articulating the business vision, involving people in how to achieve the vision, providing coaching, empowering and enhancing self-esteem and rewarding success. This not only gives people a sense of accomplishment, but also makes them feel like they are part of the company. They feel that the organization really cares about them. The more change characterizes the business, the more the business needs leadership over management.

While managers tend to develop depth of expertise in their professional discipline, leaders must develop width of experience beyond their professional disciplines. These leaders are finance professionals that assume operational responsibilities or operational managers that assume sales positions. Creating multidisciplinary task forces or small business units are great ways to develop new leaders.

Promotion to a management position is a milestone in your career. There is no promotion to leadership. Becoming a leader is a personal decision and a milestone of personal development rather than career development. The leadership milestone requires focus on three areas. First, set vision and direction toward change. Second, align people by communicating through an informal network of relationships. Third, motivate and inspire people to "buy-in" to the vision by evoking feelings, emotions and inner values.

Here is a three-step process that will accelerate your transformation from manager to leader:

First, decide to be a leader. If you have leadership traits but have not decided to lead, no matter how much you attempt to scale the corporate pinnacle, you won't reach the top. It is a decision based on desire. It is a life mission, not a job description.

Second, you have to believe you are a leader. If you do not believe in your capability to lead, you will continue to act as a manager. Imagine you are managing a department of 50 employees. You are addressing them in order to summarize the year-end report and state your expectations for the upcoming year. You can either stand there as a manager drowning in a list of Key Performance Indicators (KPIs) of employees; or you can speak to the dreams, wishes and personal expectations of the people listening to you. Believe me when I say there is a big difference!

Third, you change from management behavior to leadership behavior. An important milestone for change is when your thoughts and actions about your supporters take more time than your thoughts and actions about yourself. A leader's mind is busy with his supporter's lives. A manager's mind is busy with his own performance.

Have you noticed that leaders are dealing with supporters and not subordinates, employees or staff? Leadership is 360°. You manage employees who report to you but you lead supporters who are colleagues, managers, customers, distributors, business partners and even the Board. There is a saying that goes: "As much as the Board manages the CEO, it is the CEO who manages the Board."

The lesson is that you must see leadership beyond your reporting relationships. The 360° leader continuously inspires, motivates and influences listeners, no matter where he or she is in the corporate hierarchy.

The first thought that often comes to mind when considering change is, "What will people say?" or "How will I look?" and even, "Won't people disapprove of my new behavior?" It is most likely that they will not disapprove. However, approval or disapproval does not matter as long as your behavior is congruent with your values.

Let's wake up today to a new reality. Decide, Believe and Change. Influence the people you touch.

SET PERSONAL GOALS

Danny is the Customer Support Manager of PM Publishing in San Mateo, California. He was surprised to be promoted to this position after the previous manager resigned. Danny was not quite ready for the promotion. He had previously managed five service employees in the company's West Coast office before he was promoted to managing 36 employees in five offices nationwide.

Danny has never taken time to plan for the changes in his life. He was thrown into this situation just as he was thrown into resolving endless escalations from the regional offices. He resolves delivery delays, customer complaints, order changes and other typical service issues in the same way; always floating along in whatever direction the river of events takes him. Danny is completely reactive, struggling to manage his team and losing control of his work life. He is the last to leave every day (except for the night shift employees) and he gets home long after his kids have gone to bed. One night, while crunching on the cold dinner left behind by his wife, he wondered if there was a better way to manage his life.

Danny, like many people, has never set personal goals. For him, things just happen without a plan. It has never bothered him before, but being promoted to a leadership position left him out of his depth. He did not realize that living life without setting goals is like driving a car without knowing where to go. Danny recognized that he needs a compass to guide him in setting priorities and balancing his life.

If you want to avoid feeling out of control like Danny, it is important to set personal goals. Goals are a road map to guide us toward a destination, like a lighthouse, compass or an internal GPS.

If you're like Danny and aren't accustomed to establishing goals, the end of a year is a good time to set up goals for the following year. Most companies plan the next year at this time. It is good to align your personal goals with your corporate goals so that your career path will be congruent with your organization's path.

When I set up personal goals for the first time, I accomplished less than 10% of my goals by the end of that year. Since then my goal setting has changed dramatically. In the beginning I focused on career and prosperity. Over time, my goals evolved to include goals outside of career and prosperity.

Here are some topics to think about when setting goals:

Health

If you get sick, your set of priorities changes immediately. If you face a life threatening illness, survival becomes top priority. Prevention is important. So some sample goals for health can be:

- Exercise three times a week for 45 minutes.
- Quit smoking by dropping from one pack per day to ten cigarettes by March, five cigarettes by June, two cigarettes by September and none by December.

Relationships

Human beings are social creatures, who naturally want to improve relationships with our loved ones. Your lifestyle will occasionally stand in your way. Setting relationship goals helps to determine the changes you are looking for in your relationships. Here are some ideas:

- Get involved with your kid's school.
- Surprise your spouse with a romantic dinner at least once every 3 months.
- Get involved with your favorite charity and volunteer your time three times a year.

Leisure

Leaders work hard and play hard. It is important to take time off to re-charge. To that end, you can set goals like:

- Play tennis every Sunday.
- Take guitar lessons every Monday night.

Prosperity

Everyone would like to achieve financial freedom at one point in time (and better sooner than later). After all, if you don't save for retirement, you can never afford to retire! Saving requires planning and so you can establish goals such as:

- Allocate 20% of monthly salary to a savings account.
- Invest in rental property.

Career

You spend half of your waking time at work and definitely want to be accomplished and rewarded. This does not happen by chance. Successful career paths are planned. Where are you heading? What do you need to do to get there? These goals can be:

- Start an MBA and complete it in two years over the weekends.
- Attend a tax course to obtain a tax advisor certificate.
- Restructure department(s) to prepare for a future business expansion.

Self-Actualization

What do you feel is your true calling? It is not always easy to find the answer to this question, but one can make small movements toward it. It's helpful to spend time trying to gain clarity on the "larger questions" in your life. Some goal setting ideas might include:

- Define a purpose or framework within which you pursue all your activities.
- Define core values that drive you.

What in the world does goal setting have to do with leadership?

Leaders must first lead themselves in order to lead others. Setting goals and defining vision and values develops the inner strength that leaders require. Titles, nominations, and rankings are superficial. True leadership comes from within. Take some time to write down at least two personal goals for each of the six items above.

ACHIEVE YOUR GOALS

I was driving back home with my family on a beautiful Sunday afternoon. My thoughts began to wander, planning the New Year ahead. "I feel restless," I said. "My personal goals are not congruent."

Without hesitation my wife asked, "Are they in line with your core values?"

"My core values are still changing and I am not clear about the deepest ones," I replied.

"Just imagine what you want people to say about you after you die," she advised. It was the best advice I have ever gotten about deciding about my core values.

For a few moments I thought about my funeral. What do I want people to say about me? What legacy will I leave behind? Or in Robin Sharma's words, "Who Will Cry When You Die?" Will anyone even care about how successful I was in my job or will it be about the role I played in other people lives? Will anyone care how wealthy I was or how my wealth was used to help others?

Instead of being devastated, these thoughts gave me a fresh new perspective for goal setting. For example, I know that relationships with people is the highest priority for me. Business and career goals come second. I am not so worried about business goals as such, because successful people relationships lead to business success.

After aligning your goals to core values, it's important to align them to your business or job. Connecting goals and core values to your business gives new meaning to your job. How far can we go if our personal desires pull us in the opposite direction of our business desires? Not far! If our own values match our business values, we will rock.

Formulating goals has four steps:

1. Be specific

It is easier to achieve specific rather than general goals. For example, if you want an MBA, break it into smaller tasks: what University would you attend? Decide between an executive program or standard program; consider whether you want to pursue it on weekends or weekdays and so forth.

2. Set a time line

The reality is that most of the important goals we set are often overridden by less urgent ones. Circumstances make them lower priority and every day we have tasks that seem more important. If you do not set up a time line, another year will pass by without achieving your most important goals.

3. Write down your goals

Writing down goals is a powerful way to convert them from thoughts into a reality. Writing your goals down is a call to action.

4. Read your goals every day

Reading your goals every day triggers action. This is the art of follow up. The weeks you do not look at your goals for whatever reason are the weeks that you do not progress forward. Try writing your goals on your mobile phone to have easy access to them anytime, anywhere.

What if you do not find time to start new things?

Maria Hughes provides an answer in her book *Life's 2% Solution – Simple Steps to Achieve Happiness and Balance* (Nicholas Brealey Publishing, 2006). President of Collaborative Growth, a consulting firm for corporations and coauthor of *Emotional Intelligence in Action*, Hughes begins with a simple enough premise: setting aside 2% of personal time, or 30 minutes a day, toward examining an inner passion will lead to "a more richly textured life." This pursuit, according to Hughes, will connect you with a fundamental core self, ensure happiness and stimulate emotional and social intelligence, or EQ, which includes self-regard and empathy.

Isn't 30 minutes a day a small investment to make in pursuit of your life's goals?

VISUALIZE YOUR GAME

I pushed off the lift chair and skied slowly to the beginning of the run. I paused for a few seconds, to rapidly go over in my mind all of the new techniques I had learned in the previous three days. Lean forward, body toward downhill, hands somewhat in front, knees slightly bent, shift weight to downhill leg pressing the ski edges, uphill leg smoothly and lightly paralleling the downhill legs…there was a lot I needed to remember! Still mumbling other instructions to myself, I decisively pushed forward and began accelerating quickly down the mountain. Freezing wind and snowflakes hit my face. My mind ignored the storm while my screaming muscles fought the steep slope and rapid turns. Going over the techniques again, I struggled to stay in control of the unbelievable speed. Suddenly, the slope changed to a gentle slant approaching a chair lift. I shouted with joy…. and opened my eyes. It was dark in the room. My family was sleeping and I was in bed visualizing the following ski day.

For three days I had made progress using visualization before a ski session. Each day moved me toward better ski techniques and skills.

Visualization is a well-known technique that athletes use. Seasoned basketball, football and tennis players screen game situations in their minds before an important game. Track and field athletes visualize high jumps, distance jumps or the 100-meter sprint before they actually go on the track.

There are three types of visualizations – Have Visualization, Be Visualization and Do Visualization.

Have Visualization is visualizing what we want to have in life. It has been promoted in recent years as the "law of attraction" fad. We cannot argue with the popularity of *The Secret*. Thousands are still waiting to have their new house and car by visualizing them down to the smallest details.

Be Visualization is visualizing what you want to become. You can visualize yourself looking fit in order to get fit. You can visualize yourself appearing on TV and in magazines in order to become famous. You can visualize yourself as wealthy to get rich. The Be Visualization focuses your mind on the goals you want to achieve. It creates a clear vision of what you want to do. This vision will act as motivation, to keep you on track toward achieving that vision. This might happen as long as visualization is followed by action. Action is the only differentiator. Otherwise, Be Visualization is just a daydreaming.

Do Visualization is visualizing what you want to do. This is a no-nonsense, straightforward technique that is very powerful when you are taking action. You can take advantage of Do Visualization in order to be on top of your game, exactly like top athletes.

To champion your leadership game, you should visualize it before you take action.

I gave a speech not long ago and visualized the whole speech days before. Upon reaching the venue, I spent some time with the attendees so that I could get to know them. From the minute the speech started, my subconscious mind ran the show based on the visualization preparation while my conscious mind interacted with the listeners. No slides or notes were needed. After the speech, I checked my documents and found that not one topic was missed.

Visualization is a powerful leadership skill you can use to enhance your performance, develop capabilities, and enrich your life. More importantly, visualization enables you to make an impact on other people lives. Isn't that what good leadership all about? Visualize that.

EXCHANGE ARROGANCE FOR HUMILITY

Between 1922 and 2007, more than 13,000 people have put their lives at risk in order to pursue the dream of standing on the summit of Mount Everest. 73% of those didn't reach the summit while 208 of them died.

With so much at stake, Everest may be the best laboratory to observe arrogance and how arrogance can threaten organizations. Like the climbing teams on Everest, when a company near the top fails to make the summit, you will find leaders who think only they know what's best for their teams and organizations.

In their book *High Altitude Leadership*, Chris Warner and Don Schmincke reveal their mountaineering experiences as metaphors for leaders. With experience drawn from some of Chris's 150 brutal and most difficult mountaineering expeditions, they present a new approach to leadership.

Warner and Schmincke claim that arrogant leaders ignore warnings in boardrooms just as they do on mountaintops. They pursue their own selfish dreams, and do a lot of damage by putting others at risk—the results can be disastrous, sometimes even fatal. Arrogant leaders act as if the rules don't apply to them.

For years, I believed that charisma and confidence were important leadership virtues for me to have. One day, a colleague told me that my "confidence" was perceived by many as arrogance. This was a serious blow to my ego, along with a valuable gift of humility.

Leadership greatness can only emerge when fueled by humility.

Humility drives high performance. It improves our judgment by tempering our ego. Although we can be good and effective leaders with big egos, making the leap from good to great requires something extra. We must learn to balance our big egos with humility.

Often we don't appreciate the virtue of humility in our leaders. The most aggressive, charismatic, egocentric leaders I worked closely with in the past have all but vanished from the business arena. Most of the humble, empathic and thoughtful leaders are still at the top of their game. They are CEOs and Chairpersons of highly successful organizations.

Humility is one of the most important leadership virtues, while arrogance remains very dangerous. As a student on the climb to leadership greatness, whenever I forget to balance my ego with humility, I learn the hard way how disastrous it can be. Arrogance can and will kill you and your team, before you can even reach the summit.

STAY IN LOVE

To those who report to us, we are the most important leaders in the organization. We are more likely to influence their desire to stay or leave, their career path, ethical behavior, ability to perform well, drive to "wow" customers, job satisfaction and motivation to share the organization's vision and values.

Does this still hold true in the new corporate world of dual, triple, quadruple, or even no reporting lines?

Absolutely!

You "give" leadership like you "give" a gift. You have the most influence on the work life of people who are the closest to you. Leadership is not about position or title. Leadership is about relationships, credibility and behavior.

U.S Army Major General John H. Stanford survived the Korean and Vietnam War. He was highly decorated. The loyalty of his troops was extraordinary. Stanford later headed the Military Traffic Command for the U.S. Army during the Persian Gulf War. When he retired from the Army, he became the manager of Fulton County, GA., when Atlanta was hosting the 1996 Summer Olympics. Then, he became the superintendent of the Seattle Public Schools, where he made a big difference in public education.

When asked about how he went about developing leaders, whether in schools, the military or government, he replied:

"When anyone asks me that question, I tell them I have the secret to success in life. The secret to success is to stay in love. Staying in love gives you the fire to ignite other people. A person who is not in love doesn't really feel the kind of excitement that helps them to get ahead and lead others and to achieve. I don't know any other fire, any other thing in life that is more exhilarating and is more positive a feeling than love is."

Leadership is not an affair of the head. Leadership is an affair of the heart.

We work quite intensely and for long hours in order to do our best in high-performing organizations. We put in long hours, but it doesn't mean we can't enjoy ourselves. To persist for months and years at a demanding pace, we need the emotional fuel to replenish our spirits. We need the will to continue and the courage to do things we have never done before.

How can you encourage people's hearts? How can others encourage your hearts? How can you create a "love-ship" in your organization?

Recognizing individual contributions, good results, positive performance, special attributes, and virtues shown on the job is a great start. By putting these essentials into practice, you stimulate the internal drive within each individual and feed their spirit.

It's similar to parenting. There are two kinds of parents. The first kind mostly reprimands their kids for doing things wrong. The second kind mostly rewards their kids for doing things right.

It is the same with leaders. You want to be "hunters" of good behaviors; constantly looking for "people doing things right," telling them to "keep up the good work" and most importantly, showing appreciation publicly.

Leadership is a "love-ship"… a hunt to find and appreciate good behaviors, achievements, attitudes and values in everyone.

DARE TO CHANGE

The leader's main job is…change.

To make change happen, you must actively seek ways to make things better, to grow, innovate and improve. You need to seek out opportunities to get extraordinary things done - sometimes shaking things up. Other times you just have to grab hold of the adversity surrounding you and just make things happen. And to make new things happen, you must rely on ideas outside the boundaries of familiar experiences.

Certainty and routine breed complacency. Hardships give you the opportunity to see who you really are and what you are capable of becoming. It is essential to experiment and take risks in order to create a climate of change and renovation. It is very tough to change in times of prosperity, when people are in their comfort zone. It is easiest to change during times of adversity because crisis tends to force people to alter their behavior or course of action. Hardship doesn't leave too many choices. A crisis might come in the form of a global economic turmoil, destructive technology or other external forces. However, what about internal forces? An unexpected retirement, or the sudden passing of a charismatic founder whom the business depends heavily on, is a good example. Did the retirement of Bill Gates impact Microsoft? Sure it did. Did the death of Steve Jobs influence Apple? Simply put yes.

Is the courage to challenge and drive change, personality or behavior driven?

James M. Kouzes and Barry Z. Posner are professors at the Leavey Schools of Business, at Santa Clara University. In their book *The Leadership Challenge* (4th Edition), Kouzes and Posner argue that our behavior supports or distracts us from reaching our desired destination. The two foundations for behaviors that drive change are Purpose and Values.

If you build your house on sand, it will be unsteady. If however, you build your house on solid rock, it will survive adverse conditions. A strong sense of purpose and deeply held values form a solid rock foundation that shapes your behavior. This foundation is the compass that will direct you.

Discover Your Purpose

Call it what you want - vision, mission, legacy, dream, aspiration, or even a personal agenda – the concept is the same. If you are going to be a catalyst, you must be able to imagine a positive future. When you envision the future you want for yourself or others and feel passionate about the legacy you want to leave, you will be much more likely to take the first step forward. If you don't have the slightest clue about your hopes, dreams and aspirations, your aptitude to lead is greatly reduced, if not nullified altogether.

Discovering the central theme for your life takes time, effort and focused attention. It requires equal parts: reflecting on your past, attending to the present, pondering the future and figuring out what excites you the most. You'll know you're onto something when you begin to feel the passion.

However, here is a caveat. If your purpose is self-centered and disconnected from other people's desires, it won't be leadership. People want to hear how their hopes and dreams will make a difference. They want to see how they fit into the future you envision. Then, and only then, your purpose will touch them. By defining those things that are meaningful to everyone in the organization, you can join together with purpose and move boldly forward.

Identify Your Values

In order to stand up for your beliefs, you have to know what you care most about, what you believe in, and who you are. To earn credibility, you must first be able to clearly articulate those deeply held beliefs. Then in any challenge you face, the values will be there to point you in the right direction. When your purpose and values are shining in the darkness like a beacon, you will find the necessary courage to go against the herd. Clarity of values will give you the confidence to take charge of your life.

If you stress the principles for which you stand, people will feel your sense of purpose. If you communicate the values you hold, people who identify with those values and allow, and even welcome, your leadership.

Behavior speaks louder than words. You must model your values or risk losing credibility.

A strong foundation of purpose and values can provide you with the courage to challenge the status quo and lead change. Change cannot happen in a vacuum. Change happens when everyone holds the same sense of purpose and deeply held values. Leading change means understanding what's meaningful to others and working to align the organizational purpose with the values and dreams of everyone.

People commit to causes, not to plans. Causes lead to commitments, not KPIs.

ATTRACT SUCCESS EFFECTIVELY

In 2006, a film called *The Secret* was distributed virally through the Internet and was quickly followed by a book of the same name. In no time, *The Secret* became a cultural and social phenomenon, attracting interest from media figures such as Oprah Winfrey, Ellen DeGeneres and Larry King, as well as criticism from the mainstream press.

The Secret consists of a series of interviews related to the idea of "optimist thinking." It states that everything you want may be accomplished by wishing for it. This is called the Law of Attraction. As described in the film, the Law of Attraction principle states that feelings and thoughts can attract events, from the workings of the cosmos to the interactions among individuals in their physical, emotional, and professional affairs.

The Secret lists three required steps — "ask, believe and receive" — as the essence of the Law of Attraction:

Ask

Know what you want and ask the universe for it. This is where you need to get clear about what it is you want in order to create and visualize what you want as being as 'real' as possible.

Believe

Feel and behave as if the object of your desire is on its way. Focus your thoughts and your words on what it is you want to attract even if you have to trick yourself into believing it.

Receive

Be open to receiving it. Pay attention to your intuitive messages and signs from the Universe to help you along the way and as assurance that you are on the 'right' path. As you align yourself with the Universe and open yourself up to receiving, the very thing you want to manifest will show up.

NEW THOUGHT AND THE LAW OF ATTRACTION

Essentially, *The Secret* is touting the principles of the New Thought movement that began in the late 19th century as the historical basis for their ideas.

The idea stated in the Law of Attraction was used widely by New Thought writers. They referred to the concept that thoughts influence chance. The Law of Attraction argues that thoughts (both conscious and unconscious) can affect things outside the head, not just through motivation, but also by other means.

Various scientists have stated that many of the Law's claims are impossible, violating scientific principles and a scientific understanding of the universe. Instead, the Law may be explained as an illusion created by the connection between self-confidence and success or by one's own perception, similar to the placebo effect.

I watched *The Secret* with my family after it was released in 2007. Even my nine-year-old daughter was fascinated with the film and glued to the screen. The idea that my kids trust that all they have to do is ask, believe and receive what they want, scared me. If this were true all of us would be healthy, wealthy and successful! But this is not the case. It is a dangerous belief, and unfortunately a popular one based on the success of *The Secret*, that you just have to think about what you want to get it.

I have no doubt that positive thinking, optimism and creative visualization are important. But an important foundation for success in life is missing from *The Secret*.

Rhonda Byrne, creator of *The Secret*, told a *Newsweek* interviewer that her inspiration was her exposure to Wallace Wattles' book, *The Science of Getting Rich*. Reading this book will no doubt remind you that the key foundations for success were neglected in *The Secret*.

The first foundation: Effective Action

Wattles writes that thought is the force that causes the creative power to work for us, but we must not rely upon thought alone, ignoring action. Rather, thought and action should meet. Wattles suggests that action will be taken in a certain way. You must act effectively now!

You have to act decisively, effectively and efficiently. You don't want to procrastinate with your decisions and actions resulting from your thoughts.

There is no better time to act than now. The past is history and the future does not yet exist. You even don't have any guarantees that you will make it to the future. Every thought should be converted to action at the current moment. How many times have you told yourself, "I'll start it tomorrow, next week, next month, next year..."and you never start? When tomorrow, next week, next month or next year arrives, you were busy with something else that consumed your attention, focus and priority.

The second foundation: Enhancement

As leaders, or just human beings, your main goal is to enhance, advance and enrich every person you come in touch with. You inspire, encourage and motivate everybody around you. Everybody wants to enhance life—everybody wants more from life. You have something unique to give to somebody else, who is specifically looking for that something. You just have to make a conscious decision to act on it. Teachers, physicians, and psychologists are common professions that we most often think of as enhancing other people's lives. But it doesn't mean that each of us in our own roles of profession, family and community cannot find a way to enhance other lives.

Sure we can!

Whether you work as an accountant, in customer support, as salesperson, administrative assistant or clerk, you have something unique that can enhance, enrich and advance other peoples' lives with. If you find it, you will redefine your purpose and start a new journey toward your true-life mission, success and leadership.

EXPANSIVENESS

LEAD YOURSELF BEFORE YOU LEAD OTHERS

Do you remember the years after graduation? You were learning new skills, accumulating knowledge, becoming an expert in your field and earning a higher salary as you scaled the corporate ladder.

Your career soared until it stalled. Why?

The reason is that careers can only ride on professional knowledge for a certain distance. Sooner or later, gracefully or brutally, rapidly or slowly, you will discover that leadership is more about who you are than what you do.

Goethe wrote, "Before you can do something you must be something." You cannot be the inspirational leader you hope to be if you feel miserable and depressed. You cannot inspire people to excel if you are unmotivated. You cannot lead teams to victory if you do not feel victorious.

There is an old story that brings home this point: A father was relaxing on a couch, reading the newspaper after a long day at the office. His son began to play around him, disturbing his only peaceful moments of the day. The father, fed up, ripped out a picture of the globe that was in the paper and tore it into as many tiny pieces as he could. "Son, can you try to put this globe together?" asked the dad, hoping that this would keep the little boy busy long enough to finish reading the paper. He was stunned when his son returned after a few minutes with the globe perfectly reassembled. "How did you do it son?" asked the astonished father. The kid smiled and replied, "Daddy, on the other side of the globe there was a picture of a person. Once I got the person together, the world was okay."

Success begins within. It all starts by getting yourself together. Once you do, your own world will be okay. You will begin to see the world not as it is, but as you are. By improving, refining and defining who you are, you see the world from a more enlightened perspective.

Leadership of others begins with your own internal leadership. If you want to continue to grow, you have to continue developing yourself toward what you want to be as a human being. Self-awareness provides you with the tools to achieve your goals: in your career and in your relationships with family, friends and the community.

The key is to stop running if you are not completely clear on the ultimate destination. You may run in the wrong direction! Taking time for reflection and introspection allows you to analyze what to do and how to make continual improvements.

My personal growth starts with reading uplifting books for at least thirty minutes a day. Knowledge provides a great path to self-awareness. You are probably thinking, 'How can I find an additional 30 minutes every day to read?' Reading comes in many shapes and forms. Reading is a metaphor of gaining new knowledge on a continuous basis. Whether you read a book, listen to a MP3 audio book, attend a seminar or read an ebook on your tablet, mobile or computer; you enrich your mind.

The solution to every problem you want to solve lies within you. New knowledge will help you identify this solution and act on it. Every mistake in life has already been made by somebody else who has written about it. If you want to be a better communicator and superior parents, lovers and friends, reading and knowledge can guide you.

If you do not work from home, you probably have to commute at least 30 minutes to your workplace. Make it into your mobile university. Convert your toilet into a library. It just means making the commitment to spend some time learning something new.

The type of person you will become five years from now depends on the knowledge that you gain and the decisions you make because of this knowledge. Would you appreciate spending a few hours with Barack Obama or Bill Clinton? Do you want Dale Carnegie or Napoleon Hill to be your personal coach? Would you mind being mentored by Mahatma Gandhi and Mother Theresa? Or maybe you can learn creative thinking from Thomas Edison, Ben Franklin and Alexander Graham Bell? It's all in books.

Leaders commit to a lifetime of learning. Learning no longer ends when you finish that last exam—it must continue as long as you live. Before you lead others, you should lead yourself. Self-awareness, reflection and introspection are proven ways to know yourself and therefore become role models to the people around you, whether they are colleagues, friends, spouses or children.

EXPAND BEYOND EXPERTISE

Our life journey funnels us toward our ultimate expertise. We are programmed to become experts in one field. We start our formal education in a wide variety of subjects that narrow down to one expertise. In elementary and middle school we learn geography, art, history, physical health and many other topics. However, as we grow, the education system provides us with less width and more depth in our potential area of expertise. For example, many high school students are required to choose their tendency toward science studies focused programs or social studies focused programs. American universities define the major after the sophomore year while English universities require a decision of the major even before admission. Medical doctors start with a wide variety of sciences narrowed toward medical studies to become a general practitioner. Then, they continue the long ride toward expert certification.

Business management is no different. An accountant must be an expert in accounting. An engineer must be an expert in mechanics, electronics or other specific field. We are told that the greater our expertise, the higher we will climb the corporate ladder. Right?

Wrong!

Our expertise starts working against us in a very confusing manner. High expertise leads to professional growth and fast track career paths up to middle management. The first decade of our professional career teaches us that expertise provides a sound-track career. It is true if you want to be stuck in middle management. If you wish to grow beyond this point toward organizational leadership, then expertise works against you. It prevents you from growing to the next level for the following reasons:

- Expertise encourages a narrow view and a disconnection from the organization's other functions
- Expertise causes single-dimension problem solving because you are not aware of the impact of your expertise function on other functions
- Expertise blocks you from engaging other experts as you believe that you expertise is the crucial one (we all believe so even we don't admit it. Isn't it the reason we chose this expertise?).

It is very hard to make a conscious decision to stop doing something, which has been the key factor to our success. Isn't it? Yet, it is highly unlikely you will be promoted beyond middle management unless you change your mentality mid-career and expand your knowledge towards new areas and broader interests.

The faster you understand that the key to success lies in multi-disciplinary professional growth, the faster you will breakthrough to effective leadership in your organizations.

Most professional managers are stuck. They are locked in their expertise safe-box rather than flying out, seeking new competencies and developing inter-disciplinary knowledge. The most formal multi-disciplinary business education is a Master in Business Administration. MBA programs receive criticism for being too theoretical and less effective than businesses would like, but it is an opportunity to gain multidisciplinary business knowledge. In the past I have recommended it to colleagues. Only a few took the challenge and made the effort. Others felt that further expertise would be the key for their career path. They said that when they need complementary knowledge they would approach other experts. They didn't feel the need to learn new competencies since there were other experts they could engage on demand.

Here is the problem with that mentality. Other experts analyze issues and provide solutions without seeing the big-picture. Calling other experts to complement your single dimension expertise will eventually lead to bad decisions and higher failure rate.

An MBA is not the only way to gain multi-disciplinary competencies. Books, audios, seminars, workshops and other informal education can give you the same knowledge. It is more about changing your mentality rather than learning new topics.

Believe it or not, attending meetings with other functional experts with curiosity, and really listening and focusing on the information you learn can give you knowledge and competencies in the other areas of your organization. It's common when discussions are shifting to other areas, to divert our attention to emails, text messages or to just leave. Who hasn't thought, 'It is none of my business' and tuned out? It is probably none of your business if you want to do the same thing until you retire. It is your business if you want to become a leader.

Organizational leadership does not grow through expertise. It grows as you get involved in the broader aspects of your organization. It grows when you assume responsibilities for new functions. It grows when you expand your expertise towards new disciplines where you haven't been trained before.

Whether you are in science, business, education or any other industry, the future belongs to those who have the knowledge and depth provided by multiple disciplines. The next scientific breakthrough will come from scientists who combine biology, chemistry, physics and sciences that don't even exist yet. The next educational breakthrough will come from educators that integrate teaching with information technology (IT).

Career breakthroughs will happen when you expand your horizons and develop a multi-disciplinary approach to your career; covering all aspects of business.

LEAD WITH ADAPTIVE SKILLS

A few years ago my company's management team visited a nuclear plant. The safety briefing, the radioactivity tests and the security procedures added to the excitement of this visit. A nuclear plant is managed like no other business. A business mistake in the real world results in a loss to a company. A safety mistake in a nuclear plant results in a disaster to society. The highlight of the visit was seeing the reactor. I thought about it as a potential atomic bomb. So did the operators, who were well trained with various backup procedures aimed at preventing failures. I felt relief when we left and thought we all could learn from the excellent leaders of this industry.

Managing a nuclear facility has never been easy. It demands great technical as well as great people skills. Being a nuclear manager has always meant satisfying a variety of stakeholders, from top-level managers to a board of directors, from internal employees to outside regulators.

Jerry Yelverton is the CEO of Entergy Nuclear in the USA. Entergy operates ten nuclear plants nationwide. It has annual revenues of more than $13 billion and approximately 14,700 employees. Yelverton delivered a speech in September 15, 1997 on the topic of "Adaptive Skills." He claimed that to succeed in the demanding business environment of the nuclear power industry, managers must have two kinds of skills. "Of course, they must have top-notch technical skills. That goes without saying. But more and more, we must focus on developing the adaptive skills of our managers."

The difference between an adaptive challenge and technical challenge is simple. There are problems that are just technical. A car mechanic fixes a car or a doctor prescribes antibiotics to cure a sinus infection. Those are technical solutions. But adaptive problems demand another set of skills. Installing a new culture into a company is adaptive. There's no clear-cut technical solution. It's a challenge that is going to require people to change their values, their behaviors and their attitudes. They must be led by motivational and inspiring leaders.

Yelverton said that Entergy looked at its nuclear fleet and found out that the top performing plants were all of different technologies, designs, locations and ages. "It all comes back to the people operating them. And that all comes back to how well managers can motivate and inspire people."

The most valuable philosophy for developing managers into leaders with adaptive skills is to move them around. Don't keep them in the same department. The managers must be field tested in different roles. If a manager has just been in operations and that's all he's seen, that's a very narrow focus.

Yelverton says, "The importance of moving people around was reinforced when we interviewed 120 of Entergy's top leaders. The number one factor in their success was this: They had a variety of experiences in different functions, business units, companies, and even countries. These experiences were not your typical assignment either. These were high-risk, high visibility assignments. They were multifunctional and focused on solving a crisis or smoldering situation."

"What benefits did our 120 leaders gain from these experiences? The benefits included: They developed a better understanding of how the whole business operates; they better understood the impact of their decisions on the rest of the organization; they were able to transfer best practices to new areas; they learned how to lead in a variety of situations; plus they developed strong networks inside and outside the company…"

I personally had a career in Finance, Operations and Marketing in three different industries in three different countries. My corporate journey has included working with managers who I felt were great and those who I felt were terrible. However, all of them had qualities that helped me grow and added merit to their management styles.

Nowadays, when I encourage people to move, they sometimes say, "I don't want to work for this person." It doesn't matter whether or not you like this person. You have to look at what you can learn from him or her. Look at those behaviors you don't like and say, 'I'm not going to do some of those things.' Pick the qualities you like and incorporate them into your own emerging leadership style.

Top leaders don't wait for the assignment to come to them. They are proactive and put themselves "out there." The sooner this happens in your career, the better. Do not wait until your management moves you around. Seize the opportunity and run with it!

ENHANCE YOUR STRENGTHS

Many people assume that the path to extraordinary performance involves eliminating their weaknesses. The basic assumption is that our strengths will take care of themselves so we should focus on fixing our weaknesses.

In their new book *The Inspiring Leader,* John H. Zenger, Joseph R. Folkman and Scott K. Edinger claim that leaders who focus on their weakness zones do not improve as much. The authors reveal in their new four-year study, which involved 200,000 people that the reason for this is that when you focus on an area for improvement in which you are not interested, you are probably not so passionate about it. Don't we naturally tend to be more passionate about our strengths rather than our weaknesses? Passion is crucial for achieving significant improvement. Therefore, working on behavior which you are not interested in or passionate about will not lead to any significant changes.

I was encouraged many times to develop my weakness zones. Thirteen years ago I was applying for a CFO position for an AMEX listed company. I was asked to take a personality test, which required me to draw a tree. While analyzing the sketch, the recruiter said that my tree, which had more branches than leaves, represented my tendency towards the "big picture" rather than being detail oriented. The recruiter informed me that I don't fit a CFO role. The hiring CEO thought differently because he wanted a "big picture" CFO to drive strategic plan. I got the offer but keeping in mind my big-picture strength and detail weakness, I surrounded myself with detail-oriented professionals who compensated my weaknesses so I could focus on my strength zones.

The best leaders develop their strength zones in order to excel in their leadership roles. They do not waste too much energy on fixing weaknesses. But here is the caveat: If you strive to scale the corporate pinnacle you will have to excel in more than one competency. Studies show that the most successful leaders demonstrate three competencies: technical skills (such as strategic, financial, analytical skills, etc.), result driven orientation and people skills. If your strength is your technical core competency, growing to a higher leadership level will mean developing your people skills and improving upon your results orientation thinking as well.

There are three ways to improve your people skills: read personal development books, find a personal development coach or ask your colleagues for help. The last one is the hardest personally, but is by far the most valuable. Your perception of yourself will break while listening to the people you work with. I have tried all of them. I was lucky enough to work in a mentoring business environment where the founders found time to coach their people. I was lucky enough to have colleagues penetrate my ego "walls" in order to provide me with truthful and sometimes painful personal feedback. This took me to the next level in both my professional and personal life. When you start this journey there is no way back to your old self.

Climbing the corporate pinnacle requires tremendous people management and results orientation skills. The technical skills that you have developed throughout your career are valuable, but the best leaders trust the technical competencies of their colleagues. Surround yourself with people that are better than you in your weak technical competencies zones. Never give up developing your result orientation and people skills.

ENGAGE THE WHOLE BRAIN

Jeffery, the COO of a Fortune 500 Internet service provider (ISP), was beginning to lose patience, but then again, he has never been famous for his patience. For the last hour, he has struggled to persuade the executive team to penetrate into the Japanese market through an acquisition of a Japanese ISP.

The presentation, as usual, was perfectly manicured with lots of sales forecasts, market share data and return on investment tables. He had worked relentlessly on the presentation for the better part of a month. Jeffrey glanced nervously at his watch, realizing that his time was up and it was just one week before the next Board meeting.

Jeffery's head was filled with visions of press conferences followed by interviews with *Forbes, Financial Times*, Bloomberg, CNBC and CNN. He craved some glory after all of the blood, sweat and tears he had shed in the last three years with the company.

None of his colleagues knew all of this. In fact, they appeared indifferent to his ambitions and completely disinterested. They challenged the risks, the figures, the timing…everything. Jeffery had been so confident that nobody would disagree with this opportunity. He spent a lot of time imagining his success but he had not spent enough time on how to handle objections.

Julie, the CEO, asked for feedback and with everyone in complete agreement, decided not to pursue any further negotiations with the Japanese company. With that, the meeting came to an abrupt end.

"What went wrong?" Jeffery asked himself. He had covered every possible aspect of the acquisition. His presentation was packed with hundreds of supporting figures.

So, what did go wrong?

Jeffery, like many executives, failed to win the hearts and the minds of his team. Most of us naturally approach business presentations, public speeches, employee communications or sale pitches from the left side of our brains. We provide the facts, information, and data logically and we expect decisions, resolutions and actions based on logic.

This makes perfect sense, doesn't it?

The bad news is that logic is not always effective unless you engage the whole brain. You need to connect both the logical, analytical and objective left brain of decision makers with the emotional, creative, subjective and intuitive right brains.

Many of us are products of traditional education systems that rarely emphasize emotional engagement. We have learned to develop analytical processes in order to reach logical conclusions. Unfortunately, opinions are often formed and decisions made based on emotions rather than logic.

Your goal every time you engage an audience – colleagues, management, customers, board, or the public – is to engage the whole brain: both the left side and right side.

When you engage only the right side, nobody takes it seriously. Your communications will be nothing more than entertaining. Decisions are rarely made based on the right brain alone.

When you engage only the left side, people do not develop any feelings toward the subject and do not feel the urge to take action.

You can dramatically improve your chances of achieving results, resolutions, decisions and buy-ins from any audience by becoming whole brain leaders who engage the left and right brain in every single communication.

How do you do this?

Becoming a whole brain leader is not as complicated as it sounds. You just have to start every presentation with a message that sparks emotions with your listeners. You can build a metaphor, analogy, allegory, or any personal story with a strong message that connects the topic to the presentation.

You begin with the right brain first and then, and only then, when everyone has already emotionally engaged with the message, you switch to the left-brain and spit-out information, data, and analysis.

Finishing the informative part of the communication, you then go back to the right brain and complete the story you started and engage the audience emotionally in order to drive them to take action.

Every presentation is like a sandwich. The filling is the information between two slices of emotional engagements.

Poor Jeffery. If only he had started his presentation by sharing the same dreams he had about the glory the team should expect; if he painted the same vision of growth and how the results of the acquisition would personally affect each one of the participants, most likely he would have ended with a positive decision.

Still have doubts?

Try it the next time you are presenting information. Serve it as a sandwich of two rich emotional anecdotes with the information tightly packed within, instead of providing only the filling, spilling out all over the place.

You will get more results and you will enjoy the process, as well. If you are working on any presentations, start thinking about your emotional story and prepare to win both the minds and hearts of your audience.

UNLEASH YOUR CREATIVE POWER

There is a continuous, relentless and vicious war being waged against our creativity. Multiple email in-boxes, Facebook, LinkedIn, Twitter, YouTube, mobile texts, Skype, and WhatsApp steal our creative power. What's worse we don't even notice!

Everybody fights for our attention: our managers, colleagues, employees, advertisers, media, friends, family members and the rest of the world. They are armed and equipped with the latest technology to reach us anytime, everywhere, and anyhow.

They drive their own agendas, priorities and objectives rather than ours and they force us to be attentive and responsive within seconds. And why not? We are always connected, regardless of where we are or what we are doing. In a demanding era that requires more mindfulness, we become more mindless. The disruptors divert our focus away from our careers, businesses and personal goals toward their own careers, businesses and personal goals.

In their way, they kill our single most important success factor – creativity.

In the 21st century, creativity matters.

Creativity differentiates a successful business from a failed business. Creativity separates a successful entrepreneur from a failed entrepreneur. Creativity is the competitive advantage of every executive, entrepreneur, artist, expert and coach. Creativity is the life force that generates all the advances in our lives, from the airplanes we fly, the mobile devices we use, to the elegant cars we drive.

Do you want to be successful in life?

Then discover how to unleash your creative power!

Unleashing your creative power enables you to accomplish in life whatever you wish to. Uncreative people will most likely end up losing their jobs to people who are able to unleash their creative power.

This century belongs to the Creators.

We are all creators.

We were creative when we were children. We painted. We drew. We sculptured. We assembled. We crafted. Whether in kindergarten, on the playground, at home or at the beach, we playfully, fearlessly and imaginatively created pieces of art that our parents kept and displayed to showcase how creative we were.

- What happened to our natural flow of creativity?
- The answer is that formal education killed our creativity.
- The workplace has forced us to "fit into" standard operating procedures.
- The Internet has replaced family creative fun games.

We stopped being interested in creative, artistic and inventive imagination and started memorizing historical dates and meaningless facts in order to pass exams, score higher grades and compete with our peers.

It's time to reclaim, restore, revitalize and unleash our creativity.

But, how?

Creativity is a proactive process. You start with a decision to become a creator. Creativity requires hard work, discipline and practice—just like any other task you perform. Once you start creating, you become a creator.

Here are seven steps you can use to unleash your creativity at work, business and in every aspect of your life:

1. **Set aside a specific time frame for creativity every day.** Practice being creative each day by spending 15, 30 or even 60 minutes doing something creative. Do whatever you feel like doing. Paint, write, design, record, etc., as long as it is creative.

2. **Produce a creative outcome.** This can be whatever you naturally want to accomplish. Write a white paper, redesign your workplace, draw up a new type of process, write a poem, write a blog, or tweet a new idea. Just follow your natural calling and create something that is new and different.

3. **Practice silence.** Turn off all the noise in your life, in your mind and in your environment. Find a quiet, relaxing place and close the door. Turn off all devices – desktop, mobile, everything. Don't talk. Don't let anybody interrupt you. Just practice being silent for a few minutes each day and let your mind relax and wander.

4. **Merge your creative process with your job or business.** This means taking a creative process that you are interested in and finding a way to incorporate it into your job. For example, if you write music, offer to work on the company's next marketing video.

5. **Turn your creative time into a daily ritual.** Try to make this process into a habit. Practice and repetition are key success factors for creating a new habit. Set aside some time each and every day to practice your creativity until it becomes a habit.

6. **Dare to share.** Do something creative and then share your creative outcome with your peers, family members, friends, or…the whole world through Facebook, Tweeter or any other social media.

7. **Convert creative ideas into projects.** If you believe in your idea, ask for feedback and execute it. Don't let negative feedback get you down. Convert ideas that receive negative feedback into projects as well.

Creativity requires decision-making, time and effort just like any other task we do. Our best creative power will come from what we **want** to do rather than what we **have** to do. Allocate time, create in silence, develop your creative process, share your creative outcome and convert your creative ideas into real projects at work, business, home and life. In this way you will become a more creative person.

EXPRESS EMOTIONS

Great leaders spark new attitudes within their team members. New attitudes drive new behaviors. New behaviors result in new outcomes. Sounds simple, doesn't it? Not really. It is a very challenging aspect of leadership. Traditionally, leaders are expected to create vision, set goals and appraise performance in order to achieve results. But these practices are not effective if one important ingredient is missing.

The missing ingredient is the ability to drive emotions in people. Business schools don't teach it. CEOs don't preach it. For many years I followed leaders who were leaving their emotions at home, playing it "cool" at the office. We were role models for stifling emotions. Only recently have I learned that stirring emotions within your team makes you a better leader.

Emotions Connect You

After years of shutting down emotions at work and playing the typical detached corporate role, I realized I was just scratching the surface of my potential to influence people. I decided to unlearn this part of my corporate behavior. I discovered that being a real leader means not being afraid of sharing sorrow, caring and joy with colleagues. Sharing actually enhances rather than undermines business goals.

Over time, I have tried to exchange my previous unemotional leadership with a personally fulfilling and powerful emotional leadership. Although this has not been an easy change, it has helped in many ways. First, I don't have to play a role or wear a mask in the office. I am emotional with my wife and my kids at home. I show love, excitement, disappointment and care. Shouldn't I behave the same at work? Connecting with your true-self and letting your team "feel" you at a deeper level, allows you to really touch other people's lives, influence change and receive stronger commitments from team members.

Emotions Inspire Others

It is well known in marketing that emotions sell better than cognitive reasoning. Your chances of getting a sale are higher if you successfully evoke strong feelings in your customer. Sales people create fear when they sell insurance, appeal to greed when they sell investments or use envy to sell a luxury product. As a corporate leader, you "sell" your ideas every single day to your team. Your team members have basic needs, along with desires, aspirations and wishes. If you touch your team's hidden "buttons," you will receive greater acceptance of your ideas than just by using logic. In each and every one of us there is the little voice that asks "WITFM" (What Is There for Me?). Address this little voice and you will find your way into the heart of your team members. This makes it is easier to spark new attitudes, behaviors and outcomes.

If you wish to inspire people, genuinely express your emotions and really listen when people express theirs. Let them see your highs and lows. Excitement and enthusiasm are contagious. Be yourself, never fake. If you are grumpy today, don't say you are happy. It will be obvious. Expressing emotions truthfully allows others to know and trust you. You will know them better and hence be more effective in leading them toward fulfilling their own work, life skills and dreams.

STICK TO THE MAGIC NUMBER 3

Many people want to change jobs in order to become happier and successful. After the change, they find that they are still unhappy and unsuccessful in their new jobs. Then what? They begin the cycle again, "shopping" for the next job, believing it will ultimately make them more happy and successful. The rat race for the "perfect" job continues because they never ask, "Is it about the job or is it about me?"

New comers to an organization, at every level, tend to focus on the shortcomings of their new employer instead of their own. They do not think about the changes they need to make in order to be happy and successful. Yet, it is highly unlikely that an organization will change dramatically just to meet individual expectations. It is their own responsibility to Adopt, Adjust and Accommodate.

It is very difficult, on any rung of the corporate ladder, to do this. The more senior the position, the more difficult it is. What do these people do? Do they quit their jobs and move on to another company or do they choose to Adopt, Adjust and Accommodate?

Let me share my personal insight into this issue. After three years in each of my management positions, my effectiveness on the job escalated exponentially. Other colleagues tell me they have experienced the same thing. It's as if after a three-year milestone, one breaks through all the initial barriers and begins fulfilling their true potential.

What's so special about this milestone of three years?

After three years, you know your business model down to the smallest details. You know your customers' needs, wants and desires, and you know your markets and industry. It is a powerful combination of knowledge and experience. But above all else, it is the point when you fully assimilate your company's mission and values. You adopt them as your own. You adjust to the company culture and the unique way the business is run. You accommodate the requirements of the stakeholders – shareholders, board, and top management, etc.

For this reason, I am reluctant to hire managers that do not break through the three-year milestone. About 80% to 90% of the resumes received by my office for new management postings are from people who have spent one to two years on the job. Some people have spent only a few months in a job and are already soliciting a new one. Even more astonishing, they claim achievements that most of us cannot claim in a lifetime. Should we take these candidates seriously? Is job-hopping a life pattern that they will continue after they join us?

There are two lessons here:

The first lesson is for employees. You should stick with your employer for at least three years. During the first three years, do your utmost to Adopt, Adjust and Accommodate without losing the ability to take initiative and add value to the company. At the end of three years, you will be in a better position to judge whether your employer fits your life mission.

The second lesson is for employers. You should hire team members who have performed consistently for the same employer for more than three years. Five years is even better. These are leaders with stamina. These are leaders that will stay long enough to grow their personality and commit to the organization through time. These are leaders that will stick to it long enough to make genuine and long lasting contributions to the organization and all who work with them.

Time is value in leadership.

EFFECTIVENESS

BECOME MORE EFFECTIVE

Maria Hernandez is the best marketing talent I ever worked with. She graduated with a degree in psychology but fell in love with marketing during a summer internship while working for an advertising firm. She went back to school in order to earn an MBA. Born to a middle-class Hispanic family in Colorado, she was very proud of her Mexican heritage and had hard time leaving her family to accept an offer to relocate to South-East Asia. We worked together in Singapore for a few years and we continued to stay in-touch after our paths separated. Maria eventually moved to the UAE to work for a Marketing firm in Media City.

Naturally I wanted to meet with Maria on a trip to Dubai, and I couldn't think of a better place than the Maya Mexican restaurant, right on Jumeirah beach.

I tried to dress smarter than casual because Maria tended to overdress for any event. Her mantra has always been to keep her uniqueness all the time. She kept true to her promise and when she picked me up from my hotel, she was ready to go to a Royal Gala rather than an outdoor Mexican feast. Tall, good-looking, with dark hair with a strong square featured face, Maria is an expressive, extroverted, warm woman with a natural curiosity about people.

An hour after dinner of generous portions of food and margaritas, I learned that Maria felt that the transition from a professional position to management was not as smooth as she had expected. She struggled with delegation and editing her team's write-ups consumed most of her time. She felt that her team dragged her down more than she was able to lift up the team up.

Maria loved marketing but not marketing management. Beyond looking after her clients, which she did very well, she now had responsibilities to her firm and her team. She found she was not meeting expectations of her employer, her team and even her own self.

Many executives who take the first steps from a professional role into management don't spend enough time discerning the changes required to achieve their new goals. Maria is not an exception. She is so busy running after more daily tasks than her calendar can contain, exhausting herself and working very late hours. Being what her friends perceive as a workaholic hasn't changed anything. Maria's first conclusion was that the problem was "time management." She read the books *The Time Trap: The Classic Book on Time Management*, by Alec Mackenzie and *The Personal Efficiency Program: How to Get Organized to Do More Work in Less Time* by Kerry Gleeson. She took actions based on the books and eventually improved her efficiency, managing her outstanding tasks, replying to more emails and editing more campaigns and advertorials.

After a short time of believing she had solved the problem, Maria found herself frustrated again. Her impact on the business had not changed one bit. She didn't progress towards new strategic goals and her team started to lose faith in her leadership abilities.

Maria had a rude awakening.

Improving efficiency does not improve effectiveness.

Definitions of efficiency and effectiveness vary. My favorites are:

Efficiency means performing in the best possible manner with the least resources (i.e. time and effort).

Effectiveness means accomplishing a purpose by producing an intended result.

Being effective is about doing the right things, while being efficient is about doing things in the right way. Efficiency focuses on the process (means) whereas effectiveness focuses on achieving the (end) goal.

But here is the problem. It is much easier to improve efficiency than effectiveness because efficiency is concerned with the present while effectiveness is related to the future.

Most times being efficient requires inflexibility and following processes rigorously, and thus discourages innovation. On the other hand, being effective requires keeping the long term strategy in mind and adapting to changes quickly, thus encouraging innovation as it means thinking differently to meet a desired goal.

A big step toward leadership is putting effectiveness at a higher priority than efficiency. But this won't be enough unless you are very clear about your purpose and align your plans and actions cohesively toward a congruent direction. Then, and only then, you will impact your business and career.

The higher you scale the corporate pinnacle, the more effective you are required to become.

The opposite is also true.

The more effective you become, the higher you scale the corporate pinnacle.

So how do you become more effective?

- Define your life purpose and values.
- Set long-term goals that are aligned to your life purpose.
- Integrate your goals with your career and business.

As long as you are not crystal clear about the "right" long term goals, you will still be swimming in the muddy swamp of efficiency trying to chase the elusive holy grail of effectiveness.

My thoughts returned to the dining table where Maria was enjoying enchiladas. I shared with Maria my thoughts about effectiveness vs. efficiency and her eyes lit up.

"This is the missing part of the puzzle," Maria said. "Would you believe that strategic plans that can make a difference in my life, career and business, have been on my list for the last 18 months?"

Her eyes began to tear up. "Every single day, my most important goals and projects, the things I want to do more than anything else, are pushed aside by firefighting, urgent tasks and micro-management."

"What should I do?"

Maria's question hung in the air for a long moment.

"Focus on effectiveness, set making a long-term impact as the top priority. Everything else will follow," I replied.

"How?" Maria asked.

"It's a long answer," I smiled. "Let's order another glass of wine."

FOCUS ON 2.5%

"Do you know Vilfredo?" I asked Maria while the wine was poured into our glasses.

"No. Who is Vilferdo?

"Vilfredo Pareto," I smiled. "He was a revolutionary economist whose seminal work, *Cours d'Economie Politique*, introduced a law of income distribution, later known as Pareto's Law."

"Sure, I know. Pareto's Law demonstrates that 80% of the wealth in society is produced by 20% of the population."

It was too late to stop Maria as she continued, "Pareto showed that this 80/20 ratio could be found almost anywhere, not just in economics. For example, 80% of harvested grains were produced by 20% of the planted seeds."

"He was wrong," I laughed. "In our new economy, the 80/20 ratio is much more disproportionate."

For example, French, English and Spanish languages have about 100,000 words but 2,500 are high frequency words. If you learn how to command these 2,500 words, you will comprehend 95% of most conversations. This can be achieved in 5 months, but if you want to comprehend 98% of the vocabulary, you'll need about 5 years.

If 2.5% of the total subject matter provides 95% of the desired results, then the same 2.5% provides 3% less benefit than putting in 12 times as much effort."

"This is amazing," said Maria. "The question is: into what 2.5% should we invest our efforts?"

"Exactly," I continued. "This is our toughest challenge. Philosopher Nassim N. Taleb noted a major difference between language and business. Language is largely known but business is largely unknown. Therefore, in business 2.5% is not 2.5% of a finite knowledge but the 2.5% of what we know at the present time."

Maria got excited. "I know what 2.5% will yield my best results."

"So why don't you focus on them?"

"Because they are the least urgent and they require deep concentration, laser-beam focus and thoughtful introspection. The 2.5% lose the battle to the 97.5% putting out the fires" Maria said gloomily.

"Most people don't know what 2.5% will make a difference," I said. "I use a 'time-block' system that ensures I spend enough time and give undivided attention to discover the 2.5% most important things that will yield results and focus on doing those things."

What is the first thing you do every morning...beside brushing your teeth?" I asked.

"Check my emails...of course," Maria shot back without hesitation.

"Maria, once you start your day reading emails you lose any chance to deal with the 2.5%. You are taken over by other people's agendas. You immediately start reacting to events. Sooner or later, emails suck your morning's precious time.

Start your day with the 2.5% that matters. Discover what is the single most important thing that will make a difference and just do it. Your success factors require focus, concentration and undivided attention. The 2.5% are too comprehensive to deal with while distracted by incoming emails, phone calls, meetings and other interruptions.

Supervisory managers need no more than one hour of undivided attention, focus and concentration on their long term 2.5% to 'make a difference' goals. Middle management needs up to 2 hours and top management up to 3 hours without interruption to think, strategize, develop and innovate. The rest of the day can be left for other matters.

The 2.5% are never reactive and always proactive.

So how do you choose the 2.5%?

Reflect on your past mistakes and your visions for the future. Then, ask for feedback about those reflections from your team. If your team doesn't laugh at your goals...then the goals are not big enough.

How to work on the 2.5%?

Time Blocks.

The first 3 hours of my day (after exercising) are dedicated to business growth (strategic projects), professional growth (skills-set development) and personal growth (self-improvement).

Most of the executives tell me they don't have time for this. It will disturb "getting thing done."

They are right. They are very busy with getting things done. Some do it very efficiently but they work on the 97.5% which are not necessarily the most critical to achieve success.

The trick is to give 100% intentional focus and undivided attention to discover the 2.5% that matters and to incorporate dedicated 'time blocks' into your busy schedule to get the 2.5% done first.

I smiled as I watched Maria writing notes on the paper napkin. She always has been a lifelong learner.

REDUCE EMAILS

Jeff woke to the alarm going off on his Blackberry. With eyes half opened, he saw the 100 emails he had received during the night. He was exhausted from reading and replying to emails for more than four hours the night before. The more emails he replied to, the more emails flooded his Inbox. He took his Blackberry to the bathroom to read the latest messages, continued over breakfast and even while driving to his office. The road was jammed. His inbox was jammed. His life felt gloomy… another day of email congestion.

You might think Jeff's job title is "email responder." It isn't. Jeff is a Sales Vice President of a Multi-National Corporation. He manages 35 sales professionals across the world. He travels 60% of his time; but wherever he is or whatever he does, emails take up most of his time.

While driving to the office, Jeff thought about how things were different when he first joined the company 15 years earlier. Faxes were still the most common way to communicate with customers. Emails were sent during office hours. This all changed 12 years ago after the company gave employees laptops. In a short period of time, the volume of emails quadrupled. The email volume again grew six years ago when Blackberries arrived. Jeff's stress level has grown exponentially as he tries to cope with a communication overflow that never stops. 24 hours a day. 7 days a week. 365 days a year.

Jeff thinks, 'Communication volume is 50 times higher than 10 years ago, yet sales are at the same level. How did this happen? The number of emails shouldn't have gone from 50 to 500 per day at the same level of revenues!'

Jeff is just one of many executives who lose leadership potential because of communication overflow. The communication revolution offers us a wealth of opportunities, but it also has risks that can defeat even the most accomplished. Executives go from proactive to reactive management because of the email jam. They are not free to spend time planning for the next decade, next year, next week…or even the next day.

Have you become an "email cruncher" like Jeff?

Senior executive job descriptions do not include responding to emails. A manager who wants to grow into a leader must take control of his or her emails, not let emails take control of them. From my experience, improving email efficiency (more emails in less time) was disappointing in terms of yielding more time for leadership planning. Instead of gaining EXTRA time, the volume of emails doubled. The more rapidly I replied, the more people replied using "Reply All." The email jam became much worse.

Responding to emails is reactive management. If you as a leader do not change reactive email crunching to proactive leadership actions, you will not make a difference in your work life or in the life of your peers. You must not let emails take control of your time or your mind.

How do you change the email crunching mindset? Try avoiding emails in the morning. Use this time to be creative: to write, think, find solutions, innovate and implement. Cancel the email alert on your desktop—it is an interruption. Most of the emails are CC emails that do not require immediate attention.

Another good idea is to spend no more than 25% of your time on emails. A model for the other 75% looks like this: 25% for creative thinking, initiation, planning and solutions, 25% for personnel, coaching, meetings and management and 25% for task management and follow ups.

As the old say goes: "You cannot manage your time but you can manage yourself."

BOOST DIGITAL EFFECTIVENESS

I was excited to meet George after five years of not seeing each other. We had worked together in Hong Kong but he moved to the Middle East after five years of being my colleague. I was waiting for him at the rooftop of the recently opened Marina Bay Sands resort in Singapore when I saw his tall, tanned and confident figure looking for me at the entrance.

It took us a while to catch up with happenings of family, friends and colleagues and to enjoy the incredible view of Singapore Marina Bay at dusk, with a superb glass of wine…

Bzzzzzzzzz…

George's cellphone rang louder than an ambulance on emergency call. He impulsively picked it up, glanced at the screen for a short moment, typed quickly and placed it back on the table.

We had a few minutes of conversation about the impact of social media on future marketing when…

Bzzzzzzzzz…

George was faster than a cheetah shooting to hunt its prey. He ignored the annoyed looks from the couples around us who were trying to have a romantic dinner.

For the next 30 minutes, George received, read and responded to more messages than I took sips of wine. He was not the same guy I knew ten years ago, prior to the era of BlackBerries, iPhones, Tablets, Facebook, Twitter, LinkedIn, multiple email accounts and several mobile devices. George was disturbed, unfocused and stressed. He did not complete a full anecdote without…

Bzzzzzzzzz…

"Do you have a lot of emergencies in your business, George?" I asked patiently even though I had begun to lose my patience.

"Well, you know, the expectations are to respond to every communication at light speed, even the non- urgent messages. If I will wait for a while, other people will probably respond and take action before I am even aware. I also receive social media email alerts from my blog, LinkedIn, Facebook, Twitter, YouTube and my personal email accounts. I want to crunch them immediately before they accumulate to enormous numbers. This is life today buddy. No choice."

I was puzzled. George was a senior executive in a multi-billion dollar European telecom conglomerate. How could he manage a large organization by responding to every email, text message and social media alert with the same sense of urgency?

"How are you doing on your job, George?" I asked.

"I'm doing well but I am too busy with fire-fighting and tactical matters to deal with long term strategic matters. Information overload becomes more challenging every year. Connectivity changes the world and enables rapid response to business matters, but it is also a double-edged sword. I do not remember when the last time was I took a short break to be introspective and think. Thought processes have been replaced by overwhelming amount of communications."

I nodded my head in agreement.

I said, "A few years back we had moments when we were not reachable." We don't have that anymore. We are available 24/7 and we are expected to respond rapidly to any communication because everyone assumes that we are connected anytime and everywhere."

My sentence hung in the air because George was typing something on his mobile after another ear defeating bzzzzzzzzzzzz.

It was good timing when the bill came and it was time to say goodbye to my very distracted friend.

It got me to thinking: can senior executives be effective if they manage their communication in such a chaotic, reactive and random way?

No, they cannot.

Business leaders can lose the effectiveness battle to the misleading feeling of efficiency by reacting to the information overload that surrounds us.

What can we do? In this super connected world we have to respond to the enormous amount of communication. Don't we?

No! Not all time.

The connected world steals our inner world. It has gotten to the point where we cannot think because we are constantly listening to the noise that comes from the sources that connect us to the herd - thousands of people all the time.

You want to be in a state of mind that enables you to make the right decisions and differentiate between important matters and clatter. It is very difficult to reach a peaceful state of mind when your attention is always outward and never inward.

In order to become an effective leader, you want to enable your inward focus so that it allows you to discern the right direction.

One of my favorite stories on the meaning of peace is by an unknown author:

"There once was a king who offered a prize to the artist who would paint the best picture of peace. Many artists tried. The king looked at all the pictures. But there were only two he really liked, and he had to choose between them.

One picture was of a calm lake. The lake was a perfect mirror for peaceful towering mountains all around it. Overhead was a blue sky with fluffy white clouds. All who saw this picture thought that it was a perfect picture of peace.

The other picture had mountains, too. But these were rugged and bare. Above was an angry sky, from which rain fell and in which lightning played. Down the side of the mountain tumbled a foaming waterfall. This did not look peaceful at all.

But when the king looked closely, he saw behind the waterfall a tiny bush growing in a crack in the rock. In the bush a mother bird had built her nest. There, in the midst of the rush of angry water, sat the mother bird on her nest - in perfect peace.

Which picture do you think won the prize?

The king chose the second picture. Do you know why?

"Because," explained the king, "peace does not mean to be in a place where there is no noise, trouble, or hard work. Peace means to be in the midst of all those things and still be calm in your heart. That is the real meaning of peace."

It is the peaceful mind that develops effective leaders. Not the non-stop connectivity and instant responding to the blur of information.

You enhance your leadership effectiveness when you leave the outer world with its unstoppable demanding connectivity and enter your inner world for just a short while. In this short break you organize your thoughts and priorities and align your actions toward your goals.

ENGAGE IN EXPONENTIAL CHANGE

In the new world of exponential change the current professions, expertise, experiences and roles will be redundant faster than we can imagine. Traditional jobs as we know them will disappear from the landscape. New jobs will emerge. In this world of exponential change, leadership will be more valued than ever before. Are you ready for the new world? Let's find out...

The Experience Crash

Our experiences shape the way we lead. In a rapidly changing world, your experience becomes irrelevant or even counterproductive. Jane M. Twenge exposes in her book *Generation Me,* the enormous differences between the baby boomers, generation X (1961-1981) and generation Y (after 1981). Generation Y has a strong sense of entitlement and an unrealistic sense of possibilities. These folks are less likely to accept leadership than any previous generations because of a sense of entitlement. The individual comes first. Twenge also says that the new generation is more depressed and unfulfilled than previous ones. Imagine a workplace where we have three generations from many cultural backgrounds and numerous continents working alongside each other. We can no longer rely solely on our experience to lead.

The Expertise Crash

Business is no longer hierarchical. The new info-com revolution puts the technology at the forefront. Mass participation and collaboration through global sharing platforms make businesses more global and communal. They also change the nature of leadership from power and roles to communal collaboration.

Businesses will rely more and more on expertise beyond their organization as new mass participation, collaboration and co-creation of products and services evolve. Individuals beyond corporations provide the largest content in history (e.g. Wikipedia and YouTube). Products and services are no longer sought after within an organization. Leaders who count on expertise as their core leadership strength could become irrelevant as the world of mass collaboration, participation and co-creation reconfigures the notion of expertise.

The Control Crash

Global, collaborative and decentralized organizations are a complex system of relationships. It's more important than ever for leaders to find a way of engaging people. This spells the death of leadership as we know it, but it doesn't make it redundant. The challenge is to understand the new business landscape and how to engage the communities it forms.

Loss of control can be viewed as a threat or an opportunity. The legitimacy of structures, expertise, or roles is no longer present. The faster you adjust to the fact that positional power doesn't work, the faster you will embrace a "new age" leadership role...or mission. Leadership is more than just a job description these days. It involves every spiritual, emotional, and social dimension of your personality. It is who we are rather than what we have learned.

New Age Leadership Role

As a leader, your role is not only to get people to do, it is to get them to do more than they thought possible. The test of leadership is to make people feel stronger and more capable. As a leader, you are only as strong as your community. Facilitating culture is better than articulating strategies. A great strategy without a community with a winning spirit is doomed to fail. Adopting a sense of community will evoke the leadership style the new world is looking for.

From Position to Reputation

New Age Leadership focuses on reputation. You build a reputation by your commitment to the community rather than through personal effectiveness. Your community becomes stronger through your action as a leader. The difference between the current archaic "position of power" and new communal power is that the community needs to agree with you. Leadership has evolved from commanding leadership styles to democratic ones in the last decade of the 20th century. Leadership continues to evolve from democratic to consensus. This means you need a buy-in from all members before implementing decisions. Majority rule may try to force decisions but cannot force commitments, attitudes, motivations and obligations. You have to persuade everyone. This is consensus.

From Direction to Contribution

New leaders will be followed by using contribution rather than direction. Your style will change accordingly from a directive to a helpful style. It requires developing leadership maturity. It means being comfortable in your own skin. It means being able to see mass participation as an opportunity to create value.

From Compensation to Dedication

It is better to help individuals find opportunities to reinforce their own self-image than to reinforce performance through compensation. The reality is that people who truly love what they do will easily accept new commitments and tasks. Commitment means devotion to the organization. It means caring enough about it to maximize efforts. Being committed is about dedication. Financial rewards will not buy commitment. You have to love what you do. You have to identify yourself with your company's story.

Engagement

To build a strong community you have to engage its members. To engage members you should learn to distinguish between what matters and what doesn't to those members. You can engage by developing a story. The type of story you tell nurtures the engagement of the teams. Is the story of your department, your function, or your organization one of conflict or one of change and cooperation?

Alignment

The members of your community need to be aligned in one direction. Your role is to deploy strategies that can help bring different elements together as a whole. You can become an agent and facilitate discussions on what the community stands for. You can articulate problems the community wants to solve. It is an effort toward one cohesive direction. The way to align and build coherence is to help the participants define who they are, what they aspire to and how they hope to get there.

A New Age Leadership Pledge

I will confidently step into the future engaging the community members and aligning them toward a cohesive and worthy purpose. I will focus on tasks rather than roles. I will contribute rather than direct. I will build a reputation rather than using organizational power. Above all, I will love what I am doing and the people I am doing it with.

BECOME A LINCHPIN

Are you indispensable?

We are repeatedly told that everyone is replaceable. Is this true?

It is part of the brainwashing system that was designed 300 years ago to convert masses of people to the industrial revolution. Prior to the industrial revolution, economies were led by artists and artisans who created products. Adam Smith's *Wealth of Nations* paved the way for businesses to break production of goods into small tasks that can be carried out by low-paid people following simple instructions. Why hire highly paid, super-talented people when you can produce a thousand times more products by compliant, low-paid, replaceable people running efficient machines?

The industrial revolution represents the old economy. The new economy, which we are part of, is the information and communication revolution. The old economy advancements such as transportation, shaped our physical life. The new economy developments are transforming our intellectual life, from education, connectivity, entertainment and more. In the new economy the very last people we need on our teams are the well-paid bureaucrats, note takers, manual followers, bored laborers and fearful employees.

In the new economy we need a new type of leader. We need original thinkers, provocateurs and risk takers. We need marketers that can make human connections and passionate change agents who are willing to face rejection.

The old economy shaped our lives in a way that is contrary to the needs of the new economy. Our education systems put more effort into developing efficient, obedient subservient workers than creative, interactive, emotional and artistic contributors. Kids are a great example of how artistic creativity can be "taught out" and overtaken by obedience.

In the old economy we:

- Follow instructions
- Show up on time
- Work hard
- Suck it up

In the new economy we:

- Connect people and ideas
- Create
- Make judgment calls
- Forge new paths that have been never walked before

Seth Godin, the founder and CEO of Squidoo.com and the author of many best sellers, calls the indispensable leader a linchpin. In his book *Linchpin,* he claims that entrepreneurs and CEOs of companies like Steve Jobs at Apple, Jeff Bezos at Amazon, Mark Elliot Zuckerberg, Dustin Moskovitz, Eduardo Saverin and Chris Hughes at Facebook are linchpins in their organizations. A linchpin is an essential part of hardware. Every successful organization has at least one linchpin; some have dozens or even hundreds. The linchpin is the essential part that holds part of the operation together. Without the linchpin, it all falls apart.

Is there anyone in an organization who is totally irreplaceable? Probably not; but it is so difficult, so risky or so costly to replace linchpins, that it better not to.

What does it take to become an indispensable leader in the new economy?

Unique Art

An artist is a person with a brain for finding a new way of getting things done. An artist is a person who looks for new answers where nobody else is looking. An artist is a person who finds new connections that bring it all together and makes a difference.

This genius is within each of us, but the ways of the old economy forced our real talents aside in exchange for behaviors that really only serve to limit our ability to achieve.

You have to rediscover your natural-born instincts. You have art inside, though sometimes it's buried. It's time for you to become remarkable. Contribute. Innovate. Take a risk that might upset someone. Demonstrate initiative, innovation and insight. You will be delighted with your inner selves.

You have been trained to believe that having Unique Art is a genetic fact. It is interesting to note that our artistic interests are automatically switched on when we are kids, but tend to slowly fade away after a few years of schooling and work.

Emotional Connectivity

Most of us reserve our best emotional competencies for our private life. We rarely bring them to work. We expect to work and get paid, don't we? Shouldn't we bring our generosity, spirituality, creativity and emotions to our workplace?

The human race has learned reciprocity in order to survive. The caveman gave away something to a neighboring tribe. The other tribe reciprocated. This was how people connected millions years ago, as Marcel Mauss wrote in his research. Giving was the real power. In the caveman culture, the more we gave, the more we were perceived as powerful leaders. You have so much to give to others. You can give a smile, an encouraging word, help and sincere empathy. This is all it takes to connect emotionally with others. You are rich with free gifts to give to others.

Map-Less Navigation

What does it take to lead?

The ability to discover a path from one place to another that hasn't been paved. So many times we are waiting for someone to tell us what to do. Many times it is exactly when we shouldn't.

The biggest challenges in navigating your own way and creating your own map are the biases, expectations and experiences that shape the way you perceive the world. These perceptions might be extremely far away from reality. No one has a completely subjective view of the world. The true secret is to detach yourself of any pre-conceived notions and perceptions. This is the ability to view life without attachment. If you develop the skill to see things without attachment you will become an asset to any organization, because this is what great artists do. The diamond cutter doesn't imagine the diamond he wants. Instead, he sees the diamond that is possible by touching the stone and seeing exactly where the best lines are. No single diamond is the same as another.

Most psychologists agree that there are five traits that are essential in how people perceive us: openness, conscientiousness, extraversion, agreeableness and emotional stability. Not surprisingly, these traits are also great leadership qualities.

What does it mean for us?

If 100 years ago we needed to be able to lift heavy weight to be an asset to an organization; nowadays we have to enhance our personalities to be beneficial. In order to succeed in connecting with people, we have to develop each of the five elements. Investing time and effort to connect with people will pay off the most. Providing expertise by itself is rarely sufficient to become indispensable. Combining knowledge with smart judgment and generous contributions makes the difference. A leader who nurtures relationships is indispensable.

Bring it all together…

The indispensable leader is the one who delivers unique art, connects emotionally with others and navigates new routes by creating their own maps. The indispensable leader doesn't wait for a paralyzed crowd to figure out what to do next. The indispensable leader excels in situations of great complexity when it's impossible to follow a manual…because there is none.

Two mistakes to avoid…

Too often, great ideas are shot down in organizations. They are not rejected because they are wrong, but because the person selling them doesn't have the stature or track record to sell them. If the Financial Controller has a great marketing idea, it is better for them to sell it to the Marketing team first and let them do the selling to the rest of the organization. If a new comer were suggesting a new revolutionary strategy straight to the Board of Directors, it would be better for them to sell it to their team first or wait to gain trust and rapport at their new post. The more we focus on making changes that work down rather than up the organizational hierarchy, the better our chances to succeed in creating a new environment. Ultimately, good changes will be adopted by everyone.

MODIFY YOUR DNA

Leadership is a choice! Leadership doesn't come from titles, positions or genetics. Leaders choose to play the game, take a risk, act bold, assume responsibility and live life of passion and excitement.

The moment you realize that your leadership is a result of choices and not conditions, the effect is utterly transformational. You become more accountable and involved in closing the gap between the corporate culture you envision and the one that you currently have.

"Business as usual" is a death sentence for a business. We are living in exponential times. The top ten in-demand jobs in 2010 did not exist in 2004. If Facebook were a country, it would be the third largest in the world after China and India. The first text message was sent in December 1992. Today, the number of text messages sent and received everyday exceeds the total population of the planet. It took 38 years to reach a market audience of 50 million through radio…13 years through TV…four years through internet…three years through iPod…two years through Facebook. The amount of technical information is doubling every two years. One in eight couples married in the U.S. in 2006 met online (including yours truly). The world is changing more rapidly than any time before and it looks like the pace of change is getting faster and faster.

This is a wake-up call for every person who wants to make a difference. To be a successful business leader in the new world means to believe in changing the cultural DNA of any organization that is doing "business as usual." So what does it take to make a difference?

Be a Player

There are two kinds of participants in the new game - Players and Bystanders. The players are actively engaged in winning the game. Players bring their heart and soul to the game. They bring energy and passion to the rest of the team. They want to make a difference. Players choose to "be there." You can count on them to bring their whole self to the game.

When the game gets tougher, you find more bystanders and fewer players. The bystanders are afraid of getting hurt. Can you really be a player if you are afraid of pain? Are there any professional football players who become stars by being afraid of getting hurt? It is the same with leadership. Do not be afraid. It takes risks to be a player. Sometimes you win and sometimes you feel the pain of failure.

Take Risks

CEOs rarely complain about people who take too many risks. We have yet to hear them complain about folks pushing new initiatives, new products, new services and new revenue streams. CEOs gripe mostly about people who play it safe and avoid taking risks.

Leaders step through the door of uncertainty to seize an opportunity. Your ability to change the rules of the game is what makes the difference. This is what makes you extremely valuable. Whether it is product innovations, new strategies, advanced business systems or partnership suggestions, you can't innovate without experimenting. You can't experiment without making mistakes. You can't make mistakes unless you are willing to risk failure, which can sometimes be costly and painful.

Do you have the courage to challenge the status quo, especially if your bosses are the ones promoting the status quo? Do you have the guts to fight the bureaucracy and go beyond the boundaries of your job description?

We all face almost the same fears. Nobody is exempt. It is the ability to walk through the fear that makes the difference. Fear leads us into smaller lives. In fear we procrastinate, rationalize, paralyze, hesitate, make excuses, and ultimately end up living less fulfilling lives.

It is your own choice how to handle fear. You can feel the fear and do it anyway, or you can give in to it stop taking risks. When you walk through it, fear loses its hold. If you run from it, fear gains power. The more you walk through your fears, the more courageous you become. As a result, you become brave. You risk more. You gain self-esteem.

Making passion bigger than fear paves the way to take more risks. When you strongly believe in the significance of the outcome, when it makes a difference, when you can shout a big YES, you win over your fears.

Focus Forward

Your attitudes and motivation in the present are shaped by your view of the future. Your future isn't in the rearview mirror. Therefore, what you have done previously has nothing to do with how you are currently perceived by your peers and bosses.

Focusing forward is about elevating hope instead of thinking about past defeats.

Focusing forward enables you to change from what you have been into what you really want to accomplish.

Focusing forward is about emphasizing your strengths rather than our weaknesses. What you do right versus what you do wrong.

Focusing forward improves your problem solving capabilities.

Focusing forward makes you less defensive and more accountable. You are more likely to look in the mirror than look for someone else to blame.

Yes! You have the choice to make a difference in the world. All it takes is to be a player, take risks and focus forward. Careers can ride on professional knowledge just for a certain distance. Sooner or later, gracefully or brutally, rapidly or slowly, you will discover that leadership is more about who you are than what you do.

EMBRACE ABUNDANCE

James is a brilliant CEO. I had the chance to work closely with him years ago. He was a top graduate of an Ivy League university and acknowledged by the investment community as a sharp leader. I learned from James the importance of competitive management. James knew every single figure of his competitors' business results. He benchmarked every business parameter of his company against the competition. He highlighted the importance of gaining market share and getting a better gross profit margin than the competition. If he couldn't beat the competition…he bought them.

It was "the best way" of doing business: competitive strategy, strategic positioning, competitive advantage and core competencies. Wow! All of the buzzwords taught in business school come to life. We even practiced well-known Harvard professor Michael Porter's five forces strategy. But things got weird when James started monitoring in real time the share price of the company against the competition.

The following year, the electronic industry faced major turmoil. Our company's revenue plunged and our bottom line turned as red as blood. While we made enormous efforts to cut costs and stop the drop in our net income, James appeared at the next board meeting more confident than ever. In a dramatic speech followed by a business analysis, he claimed that the company was doing very well compared to the competition. After all, the competition lost a lot of money, too. The Board believed him. It was a convenient "truth" they wanted to adopt.

However, this did not ring true to me.

There is much more to leadership than following the competition. Competitive leadership is not effective leadership. I believe you have to innovate more than you compete.

James is still the CEO. The company has since merged with competing companies and earnings have never recovered. Meanwhile, the shares have continued to sink.

There is infinite abundance in the universe. We don't have to take from others in order to be successful. If we accept this philosophy, we focus energy away from competition and towards creativity. James has brilliance and ability. If he tunnels his talents toward creating new products, businesses and services instead of taking market share from competitors, he would add much more value to the stakeholders.

This is also true in our personal lives. You can get what you want without taking it from someone. By using your own unique perception, reasoning, imagination and intuition to enrich, you can become a creator of new ideas and profits, rather than a taker of existing ones.

Do you believe Steve Jobs spent most of his time worrying about the competition? Did he waste energy on Apple's insignificant market share? No! He focused on creating new ideas, which led to new products.

Do you believe that promotions come from competition with colleagues? Chances to be promoted come by enriching the organization as a whole, not by competing with individuals. I learned from the school of hard knocks that competition in the workplace has far less benefits than creating, advancing and developing new ideas. Promoting the team and organization is the best strategy for successful leadership.

There is abundance in the universe. Motivate others to create something out of nothing.

This is the essence of Abundance Leadership.

PART II
OUTER LEADERSHIP

DIALOGUE

MASTER COMMUNICATION

D.W. Griffith has been called "the father of film technique, the man who invented Hollywood" and "the Shakespeare of the screen." He established United Artists with Charlie Chaplin and was the first to use the phrase "Lights, Camera, Action" in 1910 on the set of *In Old California*. "Lights, Camera, Action" is still widely used in Hollywood today!

In the business world, there is a similar call to action that begins with the phrase, "Dialogue, Decision, Action."

Nothing really gets done in business, politics or communities without methodically going through a process of "Dialogue, Decision, and Action." It's quite different from a battlefield where commands are executed in split seconds. It's different from flying airplanes where swift actions can mean the difference between life and death. It's different from complicated medical surgeries when human beings' lives are at stake.

"Dialogue, Decision, Action" is a key success factor in the business world. After all, is it reasonable to expect actions when decisions are not clearly defined or are not taken?

How many times have you left a meeting with an unclear course of action that eventually led to procrastination? Or participated in the same conversation but reached different conclusions? Have you ever come out of the same meeting only to have a different understanding of the course of action required and therefore go in completely different directions?

The answer lies in engaging in dialogue that allows you to choose how to decide and then execute an agreed upon action. With these steps in place, you can avoid ineffective situations (at best) and leadership fiascos or business disasters (at worst).

Dialogue

Interestingly, Dialogue is the most important of the three. It is where we 'buy-in' or 'buy-out.' When we don't 'buy-in,' we'll naturally decide-not-to-decide and we won't take any action.

What happens in most Dialogues is that we reach the point of silence or violence. Silence feels different from violence but is actually the same. The first form is passive-aggressive and the last form is active-aggressive. Nevertheless, the end result is that the Dialogue is interrupted and the chances to make any decisions whatsoever are slim.

In their book, *Crucial Conversations – Tools for Talking When Stakes are High*, Kerry Patterson, Joseph Grenny, Ron McMillan and Al Switzler claim that people who move into silence try to avoid potential problems by withholding meaning from the Dialogue. People that move toward violence attempt to convince, control or compel others to accept their point of view.

The three most common forms of silence are masking, avoiding and withdrawing:

- **Masking** consists of understating our real opinion or presenting it in a sarcastic way so that the true meaning is hidden.
- **Avoiding** involves steering completely away from sensitive issues or "beating around the bush" without addressing the real issues.

- **Withdrawing** means pulling out of the conversation or exiting the room.

The three most common forms of violence are controlling, labeling and attacking:

- **Controlling** consists of forcing others into our way of thinking. This includes cutting others off, overstating facts, speaking in absolutes, or changing the subject abruptly when the discussion is not in our favor.
- **Labeling** tags people or ideas to create negative stereotypes so they will be dismissed and not taken seriously.
- **Attacking** includes demeaning and threatening.

Silence and violence both kill the chances to move on to the next stage of decision-making. So how do we overcome silence or violence? The authors of *Crucial Conversations* suggest that when others move to silence or violence, we have to step out of the conversation and create a comfortable, safe environment that allows everyone to share their opinions. Only then can we go back to the issue at hand and continue with a productive Dialogue.

It's not so difficult to observe people and find out who moves to silence or violence. It's much more difficult to see when we ourselves move to violence or silence. Often, we become so emotional we're not even aware that we are silent. We're not even aware that we're violent. Restoring comfort can be very difficult when we are the ones causing the problem!

Controlling Our Emotions

A proven way to control our emotions is to stop and ask ourselves questions, which will help us, get back to the Dialogue. First ask yourself these questions:

"Am I in some form of violence or silence?"

"What emotions are causing me to behave in this way?"

"What position do I take because of these emotions?"

"Do I have any facts or evidence to support my position or have I invented some assumptions?"

These questions will help you to catch and take corrective action. No one will dare continue the Dialogue until you make it safe do so.

Make It Safe

If you have lost control of your emotions, you can make it safe again by acknowledging, apologizing, smiling, or even asking for a "time-out." You make it safe by asking everyone to share his or her ideas and suggestions. You have to ask for people's opinions to get their involvement. Silence does not equal agreement.

The faster you find mutual purpose and mutual respect, the faster you clear the way toward a powerful Dialogue. Once you have effective Dialogue, Decision and Action will naturally follow.

DISCUSS BEFORE YOU DECIDE

Joan was driving home from the office when her cell phone rang. She didn't typically take calls while she was driving, but the determined caller kept ringing, so she eventually picked up.

The unusual tone of Warren's voice alarmed her.

"Joan, have you seen Ken's email?"

"No, I'm driving, Warren. Can it wait till tomorrow?"

"No!" Warren barked. "Ken just sent an email to a wide distribution that we had agreed to proceed with the China project. He instructed them to proceed with the implementation."

"Are you kidding, Warren? We actually decided to hold the project until Ken could provide a white paper summarizing the various alternatives and execution plan. The project is just not ready for implementation," Joan said.

"That was my understanding, too," replied Warren.

They both kept quiet for a moment. 'How did this happen?' thought Joan.

Joan has been the COO of Star West for almost a year. It isn't the first time she has chaired Star West's Executive Committee. And, it wasn't the first time her team left a meeting with completely different, sometimes even opposite, understandings. It wore her out!

"Are you still there?" Warren asked. Warren is Star West's constantly worried CFO. He has big concerns that things will get out of control when a large project moves forward without an official sign-off.

"Warren, I don't really get it. Wasn't it crystal clear that we support the project but we want to assess the three alternatives? Ken didn't give a presentation, a white paper summary or any kind of proposal. How could he conclude the project had been approved?"

Warren shrugged but Joan couldn't see it.

"Let's talk about it tomorrow, I will read his email tonight. Thanks for calling."

The rest of the way home, Joan silently contemplated the situation. 'What went wrong?' She thought. 'How could an agreement by the committee to continue the assessment of the project be interpreted so differently by Ken? This is a complete mess. I must clarify any misunderstandings and announce that the project is still under evaluation.

Once again, the ExCo will be perceived as a dysfunctional team. I wonder if this is a hidden agenda orchestrated by Ken? Or is it my leadership?' Joan's thoughts continued to wander while her car crawled slowly in heavy traffic over the Oakland Bay Bridge.

'Ken either has a personal agenda to manipulate the management team or his passion for the project filters out negative messages. If it is the latter, he missed the message that the project was not ready yet.'

Joan was still analyzing the communication glitch when she arrived home 30 minutes later. She thought, 'Most likely, the Dialogue was perceived by Ken as a decision because I haven't made it clear that the committee's Dialogue had not moved to a firm decision.'

The following morning began with a miserable email exchange between Joan and Ken, escalating the confusion to new levels. Ken claimed that Joan was blocking his initiatives and that they were losing precious time on non-decisive meetings. The gap between the two grew bigger and bigger.

So what's the problem, really?

Joan's team definitely doesn't realize how the decision process works. They've also come to believe that no decisions get made during long meetings. Decisions drag on forever.

These two problems require that Joan and her team decide…how to decide.

You should not allow people to assume that Dialogue is decision making. Good Dialogue encourages people to speak openly about ideas, opinions, plans and agendas. They feel safe while they are doing so and realize that it does not guarantee a resolution will be reached.

Things begin to go wrong when people's expectations are violated. They don't heartily commit to any decision if they do not understand how it was made. Managing expectations is a crucial step in the decision making process. To avoid violation of expectations, you should clearly separate Dialogue from decision. You must clearly define how decisions will be made, who will participate in the decision process and why.

CONFRONT COLLEAGUES

Joan was freezing. It was raining heavily. Everything was soaking wet. There she was, lying in bed staring up at the hole in the roof where the cold rain was soaking her.

Then Joan woke-up and realized that she had only been dreaming. But as she lay there, she began to shiver and noticed that she was drenched. The sheets were damp, but there wasn't a hole in the ceiling. Instead, Joan realized, it was a cold sweat. Shivering, Joan remembered that today was Board day. The one day she wanted to avoid more than anything else in the world.

Things had gone from bad to worse in the last 12 months since she became the COO of Star West. Sales were skiing downhill. Profits were skydiving. Cash flow had become a crash blow. The Board was beginning to lose patience.

There was also a big, dark cloud looming, which back in the day probably wouldn't be noticed. It was a miserable $3 million investment in a new home-care product that didn't meet expectations. In other words...a total loss.

In the good old days this loss would be dismissed with a notice that innovation efforts were unsuccessful...blah...blah...blah. The terrifying fact was that the first quarter net income was in the red—in the amount of $3 million. Poor Joan!

Joan was still standing in front of her bed shivering, trying to convince herself that the roof was fine. She needed to prepare for what was shaping up to be the worst day of her professional life.

She thought to herself, 'Warren was the one who lobbied heavily for this investment. I knew that the chances of this project being successful were very slim. Why didn't I stop it?'

'Why didn't I stop it?' She asked herself again later while fixing her makeup in front of the mirror.

Joan poured herself a cup of coffee and her mind began to clear. She knew the answer but refused to acknowledge it. It was the photo in the dining room that reminded her of the answer to her question. The picture of Joan and Warren smiling at the camera, was sitting on her living room shelf. It had been taken on last year's ski vacation with their families.

The truth was, Joan and Warren were best friends. They played golf together, regularly entertaining business partners and key customers every month. They spent many days traveling together on business trips. They went on vacations together. Joan's husband and Warren's wife were both IT professionals who had a lot in common. They lived in the same neighborhood and their kids studied in the same school. Joan normally thought it was great…but not this morning.

She realized with a sinking feeling that her friendship affected her leadership and ultimately Star West's business performance. She recalled some of her attempts to confront Warren's decisions in the past. Whenever she tried to confront him about issues, he became very defensive and took disagreements personally. She eventually gave-up and lived in fear that one day her inability to confront her best friend's professional decisions would damage her own career and Star West.

The fear had finally become reality. Warren had not taken any accountability for this lost investment. In fact, his emails to Board members reflected that he believed indirectly that Joan was accountable for this project, conveniently ignoring the fact that he was the major driver.

'I should have confronted him,' thought Joan as she reversed out of her garage. 'I should have confronted him,' she murmured again a few times without noticing.

Joan recalled a workshop she attended more than 10 years ago about work-life balance. It seemed like a lifetime ago! It was a different world. It was even a different century. Life is different with mobile communication and a 21st century lifestyle. 'Work is life and life is work. Separation is impossible,' thought Joan while taking the ramp to highway 24 from Walnut Creek to San Francisco.

24 miles to the office!

Joan thought about Patrick Lencioni's book, *The Five Temptations of a CEO* that she had just finished reading last week. One of the temptations was choosing popularity over accountability. 'That is exactly the problem,' thought Joan. 'I prefer to be a popular friend rather than seek accountability. We are such good friends in management, that friendship becomes more important than accountability. We even call ourselves a family- forgetting that we run a business. We behave like we don't carry responsibilities and accountabilities toward shareholders, customers, employees and our business partners.

We should not let friendships at work cloud accountability,' decided Joan conclusively. But just as she began to gain back her self-confidence, she recalled another temptation of CEOs – choosing harmony over confrontation.

Joan began to recall many situations where she avoided confronting issues she didn't agree on. In many instances, she had compromised her own beliefs and did not speak out about her disagreements. It wasn't only with Warren. It was with almost everybody. She remembered an employee joking that the management "scratched each other's backs." It was true. Harmony was definitely more important than confrontation. She even couldn't recall the last time her team had had a passionate and spirited confrontation or even an emotional outburst.

'That's over. I won't repeat this mistake again,' thought Joan. 'Friendship will never be again on the account of accountability. Friendship will not be on the account of confrontation.'

She was already on the interstate when she calculated that she would be in the office one hour before the Board meeting started. 'This will give me some time to confront Warren,' Joan thought.

She quickly dialed Warren, whose number was on speed dial. "Good morning Joan. How're you doing?" Warren greeted her warmly.

"Not so good Warren. I would like to discuss something with you before the Board meeting."

"I'm already in the office reviewing the slides. Can we do it after the Board?" Warren pleaded.

"Warren, we have to discuss it before the Board. I will be in the office in 10 minutes. See you then," she said as she hung up the call. She did not allow him time to object.

'Now, how will I confront him?' she thought.

Joan had already resolved within herself the most important reasons for her failure. She recognized that she did not confront colleagues with whom she has friendship relationships. She did not define accountabilities with her friends at work, letting accountability float without ownership.

ACQUIRE 7 CONFRONTATION RULES

Joan was anxious about how a confrontation with Warren would affect their relationship. She decided to call Brian, the consultant who delivered a communication workshop last year. He repeatedly emphasized that executives have to confront each other. Brian picked up the phone and was available to talk. After listening patiently to Joan's briefing of the situation he was ready to advise.

"Joan, it is not easy to confront colleagues, especially a friend, but it is the most rewarding process for you, for Warren and the company," said Brian. "There are 7 rules of confrontation that you have to master in order to confront effectively without negative consequences on relationships," Brian continued.

"First rule is, don't let your emotions get involved in the process. Unlike many communication experts who advise sharing emotions, I believe it will be beneficial to leave your emotional feelings outside the conversation. Confrontation with anger, frustration, doubt or fear will fail."

Joan thought it would be doubtful she could confront Warren without emotions. In fact, she'd read that it was recommended to start confrontation with how you felt about the situation. After some thought, Joan figured out why she should leave her emotions at the door. She knew that if she let her anger, disappointment and frustration sneak into the confrontation; it would heighten Warren's emotions, which might escalate into a conflict.

"Second rule is to use 'I' instead of 'you' so your counterpart will not feel defensive."

"I have never been really successful in using this technique with my husband," Joan laughed. "I use 'I' instead of 'you' as long as I'm aware of it and after a while reverse to the bad habit of 'you.' It's a very powerful technique, but a tough one."

"Third rule," Brian continued, " is to focus only on the subject matter and not to add other issues. You can lose control of the confrontation when matters from the past are brought into the discussion." Joan reminded herself to keep the confrontation only on the accountability issue related to the investment.

"Fourth rule is to listen more than you talk. The more you listen, the more effective you become at addressing the issues at stake," Brian said. Joan smiled. She had heard too many lawyers argue their point just for the point's sake.

Some of her team did it as well. She wanted to achieve collaboration rather than domination. She promised herself to listen more and talk less during the confrontation.

Joan thought that listening was one of her biggest weaknesses. She is busy all the time and her thoughts start to wander within seconds if her companion doesn't get right to the point. She knew she had a tendency to talk rather than listen.

Brian continued. "Fifth rule, be sure to confront only after you understand the other person's point of view and you reiterate it clearly."

"Right, I remember. This is an active listening technique you taught us last year, isn't it?" asked Joan. "It has worked well with my colleagues and my children too!"

"A confrontation is part of communication. If we manage our confrontations like conversations, we will easily avoid conflicts at work and at home," said Brian.

"The sixth rule is to compromise but don't give up your values. If you reach a point that you cannot compromise, state it clearly. Insist that it is an issues of values that you cannot compromise on."

"That's a great recommendation, Brian. What is the last rule?" asked Joan as she arrived at her office building.

"The seventh rule is to engage a third party if the confrontation is not resolved."

"Thank you so much Brian. That's been very helpful. Let me repeat the seven rules of confrontation to ensure that I captured them correctly:

1. Don't let your emotions be involved in the process.
2. Use 'I' instead of 'you'.
3. Focus only on the subject matter.
4. Listen more than you talk.
5. Repeat clearly the other person's point of view.
6. Compromise, but don't give up your values.
7. Engage an objective third party if you cannot resolve the matter."

"You got all of them right," said Brian. "Take care and have a great confrontation."

Joan parked her car and entered the lobby. She got into the elevator and was relieved it was empty. She didn't want to be interrupted. Even though she hadn't digested all the rules yet, she got the gist of the method. She decided to follow these rules while confronting Warren.

When the elevator door opened, she was confidant in her ability to confront Warren without letting things get out of control or seriously affect their relationship.

Joan entered the office, greeted Samantha at the reception desk and walked straight into Warren's office. She managed to evade her executive assistant Andrew's morning routine of signatures and messages.

She took a deep breath outside Warren's door and smiled while she "left her emotions at the door."

"Good morning Warren," Joan greeted with a strained smile. Her voice sounded more cheerful than she felt.

"Hello Joan," replied Warren, not even looking up. His eyes stayed glued to the monitor while typing some last minute changes to his presentation.

"Can I have your full attention, Warren?" asked Joan. She found herself disturbed with his rude reception.

'No 'I' Joan!' she scolded herself, making note of her first mistake.

Warren quickly raised his head, surprised at her tone of voice.

"Warren, we have a serious situation regarding the $3 million loss in the home-care investment. Not only that the loss is exactly the same as the company net loss, but also that we haven't discussed who is accountable for this loss." Joan took a deep breath.

Warren's face turned bright red. Joan noticed his forehead vein was popping out - his famous anger signal.

"Are you referring to me? Do you mean that I'm accountable for this loss?" Warren said in a heated tone of voice.

"You...Ah...we generally have an accountability problem in our team and specifically with this project," Joan replied, correcting quickly herself.

"Well, look who's talking. What have you taken accountability for?" Warren raised his voice higher.

Joan didn't expect such an explosion so fast. She thought that following the rules of confrontation would help calm the situation. But Warren hadn't read the rules of confrontation. She shouldn't have expected him follow the rules by: controlling his emotions, avoiding using 'I' and 'you' or sticking to the point rather than making it personal. She made a note to send the rules of confrontation to her entire team.

"Warren, we have not confronted each other enough regarding this project. The truth is, we rarely confront each other at all." Joan's voice was soft. She was proud of herself for keeping to the rules.

Warren was silent. Joan wanted to keep talking, but instead stopped herself.

'Listen more than you talk,' her inner voice whispered. She held on, waiting patiently for Warren's reply.

Warren was quiet for a while but soon said, "I thought we were on the same page all this time."

"We weren't. It was our mistake to put our relationship ahead of our responsibilities to confront each other when we disagree."

"Listen Joan, I drove the project because the product group dropped the ball. We have to discuss it further with the rest of the team. There is an accountability problem here but this project is the least of our problems. The loss in the books is a reporting issue mainly for tax purposes. We can sell the plant for a profit. It won't be the biggest issue for the Board today."

"Yes, it will," replied Joan while standing up to leave Warren's office. She glanced down at her phone and saw a text message from Andrew stating, "Where are you? The chairman is already in the boardroom." It was 8:53 and she decided to go to the boardroom to greet the chairman and the other directors. The idea that she may have resolved this project issue relaxed her a bit.

As she turned to leave, she said, "Warren, we're safe if you can convince the Board that this investment is not a total loss and it can be recovered." Joan headed to the door.

"Hold on Joan. This project is not our biggest problem!" said Warren, but it was too late. Joan was already outside the room.

She was quite confident with her new confrontation skills and feeling satisfied, vowed to use them more frequently.

BE READY FOR THE UNEXPECTED

Joan entered the boardroom with Warren following close behind on her heels. She had certainly experienced her share of bad meetings in her professional career. She did not yet know that this would be the worst one ever.

Robert Smith was the easily the most dominant person in the boardroom. He was a tall handsome man in his forties who was the founder of Star West and Chairman of the company. He was a college basketball star who had made headlines when he declined an offer to play professionally for the Los Angeles Lakers. He had decided to focus on a business he'd started during college.

"Good morning Joan and Warren," greeted Robert.

"Good morning," said Michael Johnson, the CEO of Star West and co-founder of the company. Robert and Michael had been friends since college. They played basketball together and had decided to start the business together. They had expected an IPO last year, but the growth of the company stalled. They hired Joan and began to focus on a new start up in Los Angeles.

Joan noticed a new face in the room. "Joan, Warren, allow me to introduce you to Susan. Susan Taylor is our new Board member, effective today."

"Hello Joan. Hello Warren. Nice to meet you." The three shook hands firmly.

"Let's get straight to business. I will do a formal introduction," said Robert. "Good morning Ladies and Gentlemen. I would like to open the first Board meeting of the year by introducing Susan Taylor. Susan comes to us from Goldman Sachs after deciding to move home after 10 years in Hong Kong and China…and…ah…take a break from investment banking," Robert stopped, chuckled and continued. "We are lucky to have her on board. Susan, please tell us a little about yourself."

"Good morning everyone. Thanks for the warm introduction Robbie. I am grateful for the opportunity to help you guys grow the business and support your IPO aspirations. I was born in China and immigrated to the US when I was five year old. I graduated from Princeton with a degree in Physics and have an MBA from Wharton. I start working for Goldman Sachs right after that. They relocated me to Hong Kong and then to Shanghai. I covered your industry as an analyst and later managed IPOs for Chinese and Hong Kong companies now listed on the NYSE and NASDAQ. Please don't hesitate to contact me directly. I promise to be in your face every quarter," Susan smiled.

Joan was the only person in the room that didn't laugh. Susan Taylor looked like trouble. 'At least it's only once a quarter,' thought Joan. Of course she didn't know that in just 24 hours she would see Susan all day, every day. She also didn't know that it would not be in this office. Not even in the US.

"Thanks Susan," said Robert. "You already met my partner and CEO Michael Johnson over breakfast. Michael, please introduce the executive team of Star West."

"Thanks Robert," said Michael. "On my left is Joan Wilson, the Chief Operating Officer. Joan joined us almost a year ago from our competitor. She runs the operations of Star West. She's responsible for Star West's growth both domestically and internationally, developing infrastructure, supply chains and strategic planning."

"Warren Jones is the Chief Financial Officer. Warren was the first employee of the company. He has played a critical role in our success. Warren is a details fanatic. He knows the industry inside-out and is a wizard at funding and cash flow management."

"Emma Moore is the Chief Information Officer. She turned around our management systems and led the integration of our front and back office operations."

"Alexander Miller, the CTO is responsible for product development. He successfully patented our core technology in the US and Europe."

Michael continued to introduce the rest of the executive team. "James Miller is the Vice President Sales. Samantha Anderson is the Vice President of Marketing. Ashley Jackson is the Vice President of Customer Service." Each nodded their heads as Michael introduced them.

Michael is proud of the executive team of Star West. All of them are experienced professionals and well known in the industry. But as much as all of them as individuals are stars, they have not yet performed well together as a team. The impact on the bottom line is pretty obvious. The star team of Star West was so far a losing team.

Michael opened the agenda with some remarks on the significant drop in sales and asked Warren to take it from there. Warren artfully navigated through the business results without attracting attention to the heavy losses of the project. Joan continued by presenting the growth plans in the US and Europe.

The meeting went smoothly with minimal inquiries from the others. James's presentation was weak as usual. It was obvious he was nervous. His list of accounts did not show growth and his plan to get new accounts was dull. It was Sam who saved face with a brilliant presentation of the industry, seasoned with charts and facts supporting the sharp decline of the sales in the whole industry.

Soon it was almost lunchtime. They had planned to break early because Robert had invited all of them to a basketball game between The Golden State Warriors and Houston Rockets in Oakland. Expecting heavy crowds at the arena, they intended to wrap up the meeting early.

During the presentations, Susan was writing notes but didn't ask a single question. Joan glanced at her from time to time. She noted that Susan often frowned at her notes, as if she was trying to solve a riddle. Eventually she spoke just before Robert moved to wrap-up the board meeting.

"I know I have a lot to learn about your business, so please excuse me if I jump the gun a bit," she said.

"Go ahead Susan. Feel free," Robert encouraged her. He snuck a quick look at his watch.

"Have I missed something? I cannot find any market share information in the Directors package," said Susan quietly.

There was silence in the room. Michael looked at Samantha. "Sam, do you want to take this?"

"Sure. I tried to consolidate some market information but it was unreliable. It is too premature to present invalidated data." Sam's voice didn't sound very persuasive, not even to herself.

Susan looked like a cheetah running toward its prey. "The market information is a public domain. You are right that the market volume went down last year, but how do you know you haven't lost market share to the competition?" Sam flushed red but Susan continued.

"Not only may you lose market share without even knowing it, you may build your business in low growth regions like Europe and the US, while your competitors flourish in China." Sam opened her mouth to reply but Susan wasn't finished yet.

"You are running the wrong plan at the wrong time and in the wrong place. As great as your product is, it won't save you."

You could have cut the tension in the room with a knife. The seconds of silence that followed felt like hours.

Joan was the first to break the quiet. "We have a plan for China but we deferred the presentation to the next Executive Committee because there are some technical details that have to be resolved. We are definitely clear that China is our market."

Warren joined in, "Thanks Susan. That's a valid point but we already have a plan although Joan did not present it today."

"Can you outline the plan informally?" Susan asked Joan. "We will ask to take it out of the notes and without resolutions."

Joan felt like she was about to cross a minefield. She was not emotionally prepared for this.

'Is this a trap?' she thought. But she could not ignore the challenge. In the following minutes she explained Star West's plan to relocate the China head office from Hong Kong to Guangzhou with the management and account managers, to get closer to the customers and recruit new account managers and service engineers in Guangzhou.

"Why Guangzhou?" interrupted Susan. Market reviews claim that the future growth will be in north China. Your plan doesn't cater to this growth and your operations are primarily Cantonese speakers," Susan pushed.

Joan looked at Michael and Robert, but no help came from them. James and Sam also looked paralyzed, refusing to make eye contact with her.

As much as Susan was a troublemaker, her questions were sharp and to the point. She knew the business very well. However, Joan was a skilled fighter.

"Between the choice of putting resources on forecasts that might or might not happen, we decided to put our resources where the business is right now. When the growth in the North materializes, we will assess and take action," Joan explained with an inpatient tone.

The turning point came from an unexpected direction.

"Joan, I asked Steven Chen, Taiwan country manager, to send me a plan for China and he also supports the idea to establish our China head office in the North. More specifically, Shanghai," said Robert.

"What? You asked Steven to submit a plan without informing me? This is inappropriate!" Joan felt uncomfortable confronting the chairman in front of the Board, but she felt strongly about it. "We would have asked Steven's opinion about China if we had thought it was needed. You were not transparent with us, Robert." Joan spoke sharply to her Chairman.

"You are getting too emotional about this issue Joan. Steven has known me for many years. He just offered his help."

'What a mess,' Joan thought. 'Now we have two plans. I bet Steven wants China and he plans to push Wei Ming Li, the China and Hong Kong country manager. This is unbelievable. Two country managers want China. Wei Ming plans to manage China from the South and Steven plans to take over from the North. This is not only two plans—it is also two personal agendas.'

Robert's voice cut through Joan's thoughts. "Susan suggested that you should fly to Shanghai tomorrow in order to meet with Wei Ming and Steven. She will also introduce you to some of her contacts in Shanghai."

"Well it looks like this was already set-up before the meeting, right?" asked Joan.

"Let's just say we had a long breakfast," Robert chuckled.

Joan was stunned at the unexpected trip to China. She had just acquired some confrontation skills early this morning and already would need to facilitate a confrontation between two ambitious country managers and handle a new director that was closer to the Chairman than all of the executive members. She couldn't believe that only six hours had passed since her morning dream.

Joan was also very upset about the new plan that already seemed supported by Robert and Susan. Although it was a painful experience, she successfully detached from her emotions. She was determined to make lemonade out of lemons. She would fly to China and fine-tune the plan.

What she didn't know however, was that tomorrow she would be spending 13 hours sitting next to Susan on their flight to Shanghai.

TRANSFORM INDIVIDUALS INTO TEAMS

Joan passed the security checkpoint and proceeded to the United First Class Lounge in the San Francisco International Airport. She had just found out that she would be flying to Shanghai with Susan Taylor, the new member of the Board.

'Well, Susan is not all bad news,' thought Joan joyfully. "I wouldn't fly First Class otherwise.' Susan was waiting for her at the lounge wearing a dark business suit and it looked like she was ready for a CNBC interview. Joan felt uncomfortable in her very comfortable denim jeans.

Susan waved to Joan like an old friend. "Good to see you again, Joan. Isn't it exciting? We are going to have great time in Shanghai."

Joan was not so sure, but replied, "Sure, Susan." It was only after a few more pleasantries and champagne that Susan told Joan about her childhood in China; the challenging immigration to the U.S., speaking only Mandarin and the obstacles she had overcome to get on top of the investment banking game. Joan was more reserved but reciprocated with her career and family story.

By the time the flight took off, Susan and Joan were deep in conversation. Joan's plan to get a long sleep on board was forgotten.

The food was excellent. The service was efficient without being intrusive. Two hours into the flight, Susan gently asked, "Joan, can I share with you my impressions of my first Star West board meeting?"

"Sure Susan. I would love to hear your feedback," replied Joan. To her surprise, Joan found she was excited about what Susan had to say. She had to admit that Susan was brilliant and charming. She had an ability to connect quickly and spice up a conversation with wit and wisdom. Joan felt very comfortable and glad to have her as a companion on this trip. However, this feeling didn't last long.

"I have never worked in a traditional corporate structure," Susan began. "In my investment banking career, I have spent a lot of time with CEOs and their teams. I have watched them in the most stressful moments of their business lives: Entrepreneurs trying to transform their dream start-ups into multi-billion dollar conglomerates through IPOs; CEOs who raise funds from capital markets for businesses that stop growing; executive teams that struggle to convert debt to equity. Some were successful. Some were not. It was only after a decade that I started to see patterns of success and failure in the teams that I worked with. I shared this insight with my team. As a game, we used it to predict the success or failure of an IPO or fund raising plan. We ended up with a simple, yet reliable, team assessment tool."

"What was the tool?" Joan asked eagerly.

"Hold on. The good part is yet to come," smiled Susan. "We played that game for selfish reasons. Every IPO was followed by commissions and perks. We usually managed 2 to 3 IPOs at the same time. Allocation of our time to the IPOs with the biggest chance of success was crucial for our success."

"Surprisingly, while we played 'the guess who game', we became the most successful IPO team in Goldman Sachs within a year."

"How did that happen?" asked Joan curiously.

"Well, as we discussed the weaknesses of our clients' teams, we started to avoid the same mistakes and improved our own teamwork. Imagine that we were a team of five, each having graduated top of our class from the best law, finance and business schools."

"I can imagine a collision of egos," Joan interrupted laughing.

"Exactly," Susan laughed. "There were many collisions until we witnessed brilliant teams losing their dreams because of big egos. They had much more to lose than mere commissions. They lost the once in a lifetime opportunity to have a successful IPO."

"That is painful," nodded Joan, thinking about Star West's delayed IPO that had attracted her to the company in the first place.

"When I assessed your team in yesterday's Board meeting using the same prediction tool, the result is…I predict a failing team." Susan said this with sadness in her voice.

Surprisingly Joan was not as defensive as Susan expected. "What did you see?" Joan asked.

"I saw eight individuals who work in isolation rather than as a team," Susan replied without hesitation. "When Sam, your Vice President of Marketing was not ready with the market share information, she didn't feel accountable for it and nobody else did either."

"It is her responsibility as a Vice President of Marketing, isn't it?" wondered Joan.

"No. It's the responsibility of each of you, given that market share is your key performance indicator (KPI), as it should be," Susan fired back.

Joan was now fully engaged. "With all due respect to all the work you have done in the past, I disagree with your observation." Joan's voice was becoming loud enough that most passengers turned to look at her.

"We have clear cut responsibilities and accountabilities," said Joan, quietly lowering her voice. "We define 'owner and driver' for every project, even if it falls within an individual's job description. Sam definitely has sole responsibility for market share."

"So whose problem is it that your team doesn't track market share? Does it help that you have 'drivers' but they don't get things done?" asked Susan.

Joan was silent. Susan had a good point. Owner-Driver accountability at Star West usually consisted of post mortem finger pointing rather than successful execution of growth initiatives.

"Only when the team has ownership for the results and only when the team is accountable, will the members work together to accomplish them, no matter who drives. The team members will support each other, back each other up, and compensate for each other's weaknesses." Susan was aiming straight at the problem.

"Star West's current style of 'owner-driver' accountability is doomed to fail because it supports individualism rather than teamwork. This was exactly what our team discovered working with various entrepreneurs and CEOs. As long as members are accountable for their own area of responsibility rather than that of the whole team, success is doubtful," Susan spoke thoughtfully.

Joan thought for a few seconds and pondered, "Isn't the CFO responsible for finance, the CIO for Information Technology and so on? Why should Vice President of Customer Service be responsible for market share if it falls under the VP of Marketing?"

"If you agree that market share is your company's goal, then it becomes your key performance indicator. If it's your team key performance indicator, then each one of you is accountable for market share even though it falls under the responsibility of the Marketing VP," said Susan. "So, that makes Sam the 'driver' and the team members all 'owners'."

Joan challenged Susan, "Each one of us has our own responsibilities. It is impossible to run a business when we are all accountable for everything."

"You are not all accountable for everything. You are accountable for what you agreed are the corporation's most important goals and your team's deliverables. Your accountability as a team member is to follow up with your peers on their assignments and they are accountable to follow up with you on yours. More than that; you should call them on it when they don't meet deadlines. You should push them with one hand and offer help with the other. There is nothing stronger or more powerful than peer pressure."

"I think I've got it," Joan said. "I had a confrontation with Warren, the CFO, regarding the investment in a Chinese product that hadn't done well. I called him on his accountability but felt that I was just as accountable, as was the rest of the team. Yet, we had never defined it as a team goal."

"Ambiguity in KPIs is the biggest enemy of any team. Then the team becomes just a group of individuals executing their own KPIs." Susan was amazed how fast Joan grasped the essence of the problem and reflected upon herself to make corrections.

For a few minutes Joan and Susan sat quietly. The flight attendants dimmed the lights. Each woman looked at her watch. It had been three hours since they departed and they had ten hours left before arriving in Shanghai. They decided to sleep and continue the conversation later.

Joan couldn't fall asleep. The more she thought about team ownership instead of individual ownership for tasks, goals and projects, the more it made sense to her. It meant that even performance reviews and bonuses should not be allocated solely on individual achievements but be based on the team's achievements.

United flight 857 from San Francisco to Pudong was the best business course Joan had ever taken.

PROMOTE CHANGE

Joan's heart was fluttering while "flying" from Pudong Airport at a speed of 430 km/h, hanging a few meters above the buildings. She was thrilled and disoriented, refusing to believe that she was onboard a train. The Shanghai Magnetic Levitation Train is the world's fastest ground transportation, faster than a Formula One car. She arrived at her stop in less than eight minutes and was transferred to the Grand-Hyatt. She had some time to refresh before meeting the rest of the team for dinner.

Joan stood for a few minutes staring at the magnificent view from her room on the 72nd floor. The Huangpu River cuts Shanghai into two parts and each side is a different world: the west side, Puxi, with its historical buildings and the east side, Pudong, with its impressive modern skyline. Joan was so captivated by the view that she didn't feel any jetlag. She headed to the river to take a walk and organize her thoughts. She had learned a lot on the flight over, and now she was about to learn another important leadership lesson.

The Bund River Promenade at sunset was crowded with tourists, vendors and strollers who were not bothered by the chilly breeze. Joan reflected as she walked. She made the decision to avoid business discussions at dinner. There are would be two intensive days in which to finalize their China plan. Then Susan, the newest Board member, would coordinate two days of meetings with government officials and potential business partners.

Joan considered the two different plans created by her two co-workers, to introduce the company's new Chinese business plan. Her team's efforts ended with a plan to develop the market in southern China to be managed by Hong Kong General Manager Wei Ming. An alternative plan was designed by the ambitious Taiwan General Manger, Ying Ping, who believed that northern China would be a better market. Both Wei Ming and Ying Ping are at the ready with tons of slides, charts and research to support their opinions.

'The problem is that everyone knows I support the southern China plan,' thought Joan. This put her in the position of being biased toward one side. 'Is this the reason Susan became involved?' Joan wondered aloud.

As she walked, she considered a few things about herself. Joan feels that the biggest mistakes she has made during her transformation from functional to general management has been to take a stand before knowing all the information. She has also had difficulty dealing with new information that might affect decision-making. She makes a mental note to herself: Review new information without holding onto love for previous ones.

Change is tough!

Joan truly believes in the original plan for southern China. It was backed by most of Star West's clients in southern China. However, many of the Board members think differently and she will have to deal with it.

She says aloud to no one, "How can I avoid the personal agenda of Wei Ming who wants to move to Guangzhou or that of Ying Ping who wants to move to Shanghai?"

Wei Ming is a reserved and articulate executive who had a great career in sales before joining Star West two years ago. Ying Ping is exactly the opposite. She is emotional, outspoken and a great communicator, but less organized than Wei Ming. She joined Star West also two years ago, after 20 years in software marketing to the electronic industry.

Joan's thoughts race ahead. If two managers promote two different plans, then when we decide to implement one plan the promoter of this plan wins and the promoter of the other plan loses. Can we afford to have one feel like a "loser"? Will the "loser" contribute with the same passion, and dedication he/she would contribute to their own plan? Joan has debated this very issue since she became COO. In this job, she needs a cross-functional viewpoint instead of a single business dimension that finance, operations or marketing managers normally have.

This is a typical transition that functional managers need to make to be successful in general management roles. They have to grow to see the various aspects of the business and support decisions that can be contrary to their functional role. If, for example, CFOs look only at cost saving in every business decision in the way they do as Financial Controllers, they miss the opportunity to drive business as part of the general management team.

Joan reached the end of the Bund Promenade and turned back. She decided to erase her original plans, decisions and beliefs. She wants to facilitate the decision process without prejudgments.

However...

How can she direct two people who hold conflicting opinions? People are reluctant to surrender old beliefs. They tend to use new ideas to validate existing beliefs.

Joan was concentrating so much on her dilemma that she didn't notice that people were looking at her while she spoke aloud to herself while walking in the crowd.

Joan wondered if there is a third plan which could combine both the northern and southern plans. Joan startled the people next to her by speaking excitedly, "I got it!" she says aloud. She thinks, 'If we derive a new plan from the two existing ones using the advantages and removing the disadvantages, we will have a plan where everyone wins. We can expand the north and south at the same time and take advantage of the experience of both Wei Ming and Ying Ping.' With a loud "YES!" she high-fives the air, while the crowd around her smiles; caught up in her excitement.

At that point Joan begins to believe that she will successfully merge two directions into one plan. Now, Joan was excited to meet her colleagues. Tonight she will enjoy herself...no business talk!

ENGAGE TO GET COMMITMENT

It was already noon. The meeting had been going on for more than three hours without meaningful progress or signals of what might be a good course of action.

Joan felt that she had lost control of the meeting. Wei Ming, the Hong Kong General Manager, bored them with a long and overly detailed presentation of the Mainland Chinese market. He did not smile once. He slid his hand frequently through his thick black hair, staring at the screen where he projected his slides as if nobody was in the Boardroom. Wei Ming acted as if they were wasting his precious time. His South-China plan was a done deal. At least, this is what he thought.

Ying Ping, the Taiwan General Manager followed him, trying harder to engage and entertain. Her much lighter presentation focused on the expected high growth in North-China, but it also failed to attract attention from the participants. Neither speaker offered any new information nor did they attempt to bridge the gap between the two plans. Even the usually charming Ying Ping skipped making eye contact with Wei Ming.

Wei Ming kept himself busy with an impressive collection of what seemed like the latest mobile gadgets. A Macbook Air, an iPad, an Android tablet and two smartphones kept him fully occupied with everything except the discussion.

Joan stared for a few long moments through the window of the 53rd floor Boardroom of the Grand Hyatt Pudong at the breathtaking view. She noticed that everybody was texting, browsing, or emailing rather than engaging in productive discussion. She announced the lunch break and stayed behind to organize her thoughts.

Joan knows she has to get commitment for one plan. It won't happen without active discussion during which the pros and cons of each option will be considered carefully. No more monologues. Everyone is so wrapped up in their own "wired" world that there doesn't seem to be engagement during meetings. She was astonished yesterday when during dinner everyone was so busy connecting with the rest of the world but not with the people sitting around the table. Mobile technology does not support building relationships.

It has to be stopped during meetings!

They came back from lunch and Joan was ready with the new rules of engagement. "We have spent the whole morning without reaching any resolution or even clarity of the business direction," she opened. "Our business won't fall apart if we disconnect for the rest of the day. Please turn off all of your communication devices – tablets, smartphones, and laptops – and let's get down to business."

"I cannot turn off my mobile devices," Wei Ming said impatiently. "I am expecting a notice from China Telecom regarding the software contract."

"Wei Ming, would you lose the deal if you were flying 13 hours to the US?" asked Joan.

Wei Ming didn't reply. He had never seen Joan so decisive and determined.

"Is this meeting important to you?" asked Joan.

She noticed everyone's head nod in agreement.

"Then let's treat this meeting with respect and reach consensus on the business plan."

"We cannot reach consensus," said Ying Ping. "Our business assumptions are too wide apart."

"So let's narrow the gaps. Wei Ming, please present Ying Ping's plan. Ying Ping, please present Wei Ming's plan. Each of you focus on the pros of the opposite plan."

"There aren't any pros in Wei Ming's plan!" Ying Ping erupted.

"That is what you think. Please present the pros that he suggested. Only by showing that you listened carefully to the opposite opinion, have understood it fully and asked clarifying questions, have you earned the right to object. You don't earn the right to object before you show that you can present the positive side of your counter plan. Does that make sense?"

There was silence in the Boardroom. Everyone look at each other with what Joan felt was shame.

"I agree," announced Warren, the CFO, turning off his tablet with an exaggerated movement and put it in his bag.

The rest followed within seconds, even Wei Ming did reluctantly.

It was a turning point in the meeting. Everyone engaged in passionate conversation. Not surprisingly Wei Ming and Yong Ping had difficulties reiterating the opposite plan's pros. In the next two hours they tried to challenge each other plan's strengths. By 4:00 pm it was clear to everyone that both plans were viable and each plan had advantages and disadvantages.

It was James Miller, the Vice President of Sales, who broke into the discussion by asking, "Can we integrate the North-China plan with the South-China plan?"

"Right!" added Samantha Anderson, the Vice President Marketing. "We keep the strengths and eliminate the weaknesses of both plans."

"Warren, wouldn't that increase our overheads significantly?" asked Joan.

"Not really. The overheads won't be high if we open two modest offices and engage shared services in finance and marketing. It is actually a brilliant idea," replied Warren.

Everyone got excited except Wei Ming and Ying Ping. "What do you think?" Joan asked as she turned to them.

"Who will be the leader of China? We need one General Manager. China is one country. I am supposed to relocate to Shanghai to lead the market. Where do I stand in a combined plan?"

"That's a valid point, Wei Ming but let's leave the personal decisions for later on and agree first on the solution," said Joan.

"It's not personal," Wei Ming responded irritated. "We shouldn't differentiate leadership from the solution. The real decision is who will be the leader."

Joan observed Ying Ping turning red. Then she exploded without noticing that she was speaking Chinese, "It's all about you and your ego. Isn't it?"

"Hold on," Joan intervened. "Let's stick to the solution...and to English," she smiled. "The decision regarding leadership is important and we will not avoid it. Do you have objections to two business centers, one in Guangzhou and one in Shanghai?"

Joan spent the next 30 minutes asking each participant for objections, clarifications and commitment for execution.

This is the step most executives skip and what comes back to haunt them when plans are executed. There are always key players that do not support the plan and do not reveal their objections. Instead they passively don't go the extra mile needed to implement agreed plans. Most business plans require that extra mile. If individuals don't support the plan, they will eventually fail their teams 'innocently', 'nonchalantly' and 'inattentively'. These are the most dangerous players in corporate teams. They don't offer their objections before a decision is reached and then react negatively because they don't support it. Joan didn't want this to happen. She looked into the eyes of each one of players when she asked for objections, concerns and commitments. The verbal commitment was more important than the signed resolution.

Wei Ming and Ying Ping were still hesitating. It was only after they were guaranteed inclusion in the leadership plan that they admitted that from a business perspective, it was a good plan and they would support its execution.

They had a coffee break and Joan took the opportunity to offer Wei Ming and Ying Ping co-leadership positions. They would both be relocated to China, incorporate a new company, become the directors and hire a new local Mainland Chinese General Manager. They both agreed on the spot.

An hour later, they summarized the plan and the action items and left for their rooms. Tomorrow they would prepare the execution plan.

Joan was exhausted but satisfied. She called Michael Johnson, the CEO, and briefed him on the results of the meeting.

"Good work Joan. It's a good plan and as long as everybody is on board, I believe it will turn around our business. Have a good night." Michael could not see Joan's big smile in response.

CONDUCT REALITY CHECKS

What is the key to making a Dialogue genuine and honest?

You have learned from experience that implementing a plan can be a tentative experience unless key individuals bring into the Dialogue their various, sometimes conflicting, opinions and realities. Unless the realities of these key individuals are explored, you will spend a lot of time, money, energy and emotions to clean up the mess of plans that were rejected by these individuals. They will resent your plans because their personal experiences, knowledge and beliefs were not taken into account when you decided to turn plans into actions.

When you make a proposal, suggest a course of action or brainstorm solutions, you are risking failure if you make a decision before you explore the realities of all of the key individuals involved.

Why do you need to discover everyone's reality? Wouldn't everyone speak out about his or her feelings without being asked? Although they might, many are knowledgeable but afraid to introduce a controversial opinion or are silent because they have a different personal agenda. As leaders, before you move into the decision process, you should check individually for understanding and agreement.

Check for Understanding

To check for understanding simply means to invite questions and clarifications. Just asking, "What do you think?" is not a check for understanding. You ask specifically for clarifying questions and if a person is silent or seems confused, you approach him or her directly. For example, ask, "Melinda, what questions do you have?"

Check for Agreement

Once you are certain that everyone understands the proposal, you can check for agreement. You can say, "Before we move forward to make a decision about the right course of action, some of you may see it differently. If you do, please speak out. My enthusiasm may make it hard for you to challenge this, but we need your input to make the right decision for the organization."

When this approach does not work, and sometimes it doesn't, you ask every individual at the table personally for their opinion. For example, "Mitch, what's your perspective on this?" Silent individuals are more dangerous to the process than vocal ones. Every individual involved in the process should feel safe and encouraged to express his/her agreement or objection.

Personal requests work better because you publicly and openly invite people to challenge you. When you encourage people to actively share opposing views, you show that you are open to rational influence – that their feelings and opinions matter. Then, you can continue the process following the sharing of others' ideas. "Paul, what is your perspective on Mitch's idea?"

Susan Scott explains in her book *Fierce Conversations*, the "Mineral Rights" conversation model. "If you're drilling for water, it's better to drill one 100-foot well than 100 one-foot wells." This kind of conversation interrogates reality by mining for increased clarity, improved understanding and driven change.

The Mineral Rights conversation ensures that you question reality and perspective in a way that doesn't miss hidden agendas, unexplored options and resentful individuals.

It is not as easy as it sounds. Often, we fall prey to our emotions, agendas, fear of resentment and the "need" to be right. You can stop this uncontrolled tendency. You can change your communication styles by continually asking yourself questions. These questions will help you detach from negative emotions and perpetuate the process of identifying reality.

Some of the questions you can ask yourself are: What is the most important thing? What is the underlying issue? What are the current results? What is at stake if nothing changes? What is my contribution to the situation? What is the ideal outcome? What's the next step?

By questioning yourself, you can stop drifting into emotional rants during crucial conversations. Asking questions helps continue the process of understanding other people's views and seeking agreement, while enriching relationships and enhancing learning.

NAVIGATE THE INFORMAL ORGANIZATION

What happens outside of the organizational structure is often more important than what happens within. If you have been trained, like me, in the hard disciplines of finance, operations or technology management, you probably tend to work most naturally through tangibles like organization charts, process flows, scorecards, and Key Performance Indicators (KPIs).

Even though we recognize the importance of the intangibles like informal networks, relationships, cultural norms, emotional realities and peer pressure, we tend to underestimate the importance of leading beyond the tangibles. In today's business environment of rapid change, increasing globalization and web-based social networks, more companies nurture all kinds of informal and non-hierarchical relationships rather than relying solely on formal rules of engagement.

At work are two different organizations. The "formal organization" is the management structure: processes, procedures, performance metrics and formal strategies. The "informal organization" is the culture: social networks, peer interactions and communities. We know the formal organization but the key to success is to master the informal one and integrate it into the formal so they will coherently affect each other.

Ignoring elements that operate informally is a recipe for leadership failure. Ignoring the thread of culture, values and relationships by calling them "politics" is like being a person with strong cognitive skills and a weak emotional dimension. What happens informally in our organizations has more impact than what is said and done in the boardroom.

It is not easy to make a shift towards the informal. It demands more of our real selves and less of our professional persona. It is worth making the effort. You can be on top of the game if you provide emotional support, take advantage of the flexibility and speed of social networks, connect with people informally, and motivate through emotions.

You may feel at ease with formal mechanisms because they are definitive. Informal mechanisms aren't concrete and measurable. Informal elements influence behavior primarily thorough emotional means.

Integrating informal and formal mechanisms is tricky. After years of negative perceptions regarding informal organizational networks, from "politics" through "pantry talks" to "rumors," integrating the informal and the formal is a paradigm shift in leadership behavior. Here are some of the ways you can effectively integrate the two organizations:

Drive Emotions into Strategic Plans

Presenting strategic plans, even when they are signed off by the Board of Directors, does not guarantee a buy-in. You will more likely motivate people if you touch their emotions and excite imaginations by discussing how the plan will affect their personal and work life.

Form Work Groups Based on Communities

Support of your plans may come from the least expected people. Some of them may even be outside your reporting lines, departments or even the organization.

Offer Value to Satisfy People with Different Ambitions

People have agendas. It is not enough to count on the formal organization to direct ambitions toward a desired direction. "What is there for me?" is the question lurking in the subconscious mind. When you provide value to build interest in your plans, projects or initiatives, you align the corporate needs with personal needs. You want people to feel connected, involved, appreciated and proud of what they are doing.

Enhance Motivation through Pride

One of the strongest positive emotional drivers is pride. Pride in the journey can be as motivating as pride in the destination. Studies show that how people feel about their work and the pride they take in their accomplishments can be as powerful as the formal rewards of money and promotions. Pride is at the heart of what motivates the best performers.

Stimulate Performance with Values

Two organizations posted their values on their websites, manuals and flyers. The first organization's values were communication, respect, integrity and excellence. Employees' surveys showed they supported these values – because who could disagree with any of those words? However, they didn't apply them.

The second organization's values were honor, courage and commitment. People in this organization make daily critical decisions based on those principles.

The first organization was Enron, which went bankrupt after massive accounting irregularities in 2001. The second organization is the U.S. Navy. The critical difference between these organizations is that Enron was a values-displayed organization where values were nothing but words on paper. The U.S. Navy is a value-driven organization, in which values serve to guide day-to-day actions and decisions.

The informal organization is responsible for elevating values from admirable statements into a way of life. In value-driven organizations, values are shared by people who act consistently upon them.

It all boils down to paying attention to the informal elements of your organization. You can improve your organizational effectiveness and performance significantly better by learning how to connect emotionally as well as rationally with more of your colleagues.

If you put in place new formalities to address an operational challenge, yet are not getting the needed behavior, then you probably have to make more efforts to influence and energize the informal organization and integrate it with the formal one.

STEP AWAY FROM THE POWER POINT

Michelle was presenting her ideas for improvement of the integrated system of the business she works for. She covered all the changes needed in the processes, systems, people skills and resources. Sadly, no one was listening. Most of her colleagues, like thieves in the night, were text messaging under the desk, while cautiously glancing around to make sure no one was watching them.

Everyone was busy while poor Michelle was pitching her slides; each packed with too much small print and too many lines. Michelle continued her cumbersome presentation, pretending that everything was "business as usual," reading the slides with her back to the audience. She turned to the listeners from time to time, as if she was wondering if the people were still there before turning back to the screen.

Have you been in this situation before? I bet you have. I have been there, too. For the last ten years, I have been a Power Point freak. Every idea, even simple ones, was carefully crafted into too many slides. Sometimes my presentations had more than 100 slides. Through the years I became so good at preparing presentations that it took only one hour to prepare a complete presentation from scratch. Microsoft should have chosen me to be a product ambassador!

Reading *Real Leaders Don't Do Power Point,* by Christopher Witt changed my mind. This book is a "must read" for every leader who wants to powerfully get their ideas across. Witt's premise is that Power Point presentations direct the audience's attention to the screen… instead of to the presenter. The speaker tells the story, the slides don't.

Alas, many managers have become dependent on Power Point. If the projector stops working, they stop talking. The message they had to give gets buried along with the non-presented slides. The way to stop the Power Point addiction is to follow this simple plan:

Tell them what you're going to say. Say it. Tell them what you said.

The way to do this is to have one Big Idea. Crystallize your thoughts into a single idea and present it clearly and concisely. Then, develop three elements that support the Big Idea. Talk about each of the three elements and how they relate to the Big Idea. Add evidence, anecdotes or stories and wrap it up with a call for action.

This method is a powerful way to transform a boring presentation into an inspiring speech. Last week I gave a speech in India. A Power Point from the "old days" was ready. Although, the comfort of the projector in the meeting room was inviting, I overcame my addiction. Opening with the Big Idea, I shared an emotional story, developed three elements to support the Big Idea and concluded with a summary of the Big Idea and finished with a call for action.

Of course, a good speech is short. Longer than 20 minutes is too long. The best speeches made by talented speakers are usually about seven to ten minutes long. The ability to deliver your message in a concise way is a skill every inspirational speaker needs.

Would I ever use a Power Point again? Yes, but only for visual information, such as marketing charts, financial reports, sales figures, system architecture, etc. For inspirational, motivational or persuasive topics - Power Point is not an option.

Remember that a Power Point slide directs attention towards the screen and not towards you. You lose your audience with every slide. If you do use a slide, show it, talk about it and then click "B" to blacken the screen. Continue to talk until you need to show another slide. Also, ask somebody to change slides for you, so you don't have to look at the screen.

It takes a lot longer to prepare a good speech than it takes to prepare a Power Point. You have to write the Big Idea, memorize the elements and rehearse. It's important for the speech to have an impact so that the audience takes action. It is hard work. But it is very powerful and very rewarding too.

PAY ATTENTION

The last decade has revolutionized our lives, hasn't it?

In just 10 years we have wired ourselves to the world anywhere, anytime. We create, build and join large communities in a matter of seconds. We can reach, talk, see and connect with friends, colleagues and partners in real-time. We can virtually be present in meetings in several continents at the same time – as long as we have an Internet connection.

The 20th century revolutionized our lives in the way we commute. Jet planes, magnetic trains and reliable cars have enabled us to physically transport from place to place quickly enough to attend events at the opposite sides of earth in the same day.

The 21st century has revolutionized our lives in the way in which we communicate. Internet technology enables us to be virtually at the same time in many places, communicating with people and communities in split seconds.

There was also a quiet change in the way we LOVE.

In the 20th century, the currency of love and friendship was attendance. When we spent time with our loved ones doing things together, it was an act of love. In the nineties, we used to say that we spent quality time with our kids; on the playground, at home, or at dinner – we were there, fully attending and paying attention.

This all changed in the 21st century. Since the arrival of the Internet revolution, attendance does not necessarily mean attention. We physically attend activities with our loved ones while our mobile devices are connected to thousands or even millions who steal our attention. Connected to email, social networks and micro blogs, we are virtually everywhere at the same time, except for the people we are physically with.

Attendance does not necessarily mean attention. Attendance means nothing anymore. We have dinner with our loved ones while we are glancing at mobile screens, reading instant messages. Emails reach us in real time demanding immediate responses.

What's next? Are we going to soon see waterproof mobile devices to use while showering or swimming? Will we use brain chips to reply to emails while we are sleeping?

Our loved ones scream for our undivided attention. In other words, they want us to be truly connected physically and intellectually, instead of virtually.

Our kids, parents, siblings, spouses and friends want us to be there for them fully, in mind body and spirit rather than with thousands of other unknown people.

Our real friends are not the illusive thousands in our Facebook account but those that are really close to us. They may even have troubles that we do not notice because of the constant noise of the wired world.

Love has changed its currency. "Wired" attendance is not enough to build relationships. Attention is needed to build real, lasting love and friendship.

When we are with our loved-ones and we want to love and be loved, we have to turn off the electronic devices and fully attend the moment with our spouses, kids, colleagues and friends. These are the people who help us create a meaningful and fulfilling life.

Attention is the new currency of love.

DECISION

DECIDE HOW TO DECIDE

There are four common methods of decision-making:

Command

Command decision-making doesn't involve others in the decision. We just give an order to somebody or receive an order from somebody. When we receive a command decision, we can clarify what elements are flexible and what elements are not flexible. When we give a top-down order, we can explain the reason for the command. The accountability lies with the command decision maker. 'Buy-in' does not exist. Commitment may or may not be there. The higher in the corporate hierarchy a command decision is taken, the lower the chances of good execution are.

Consult

We make consult decisions when we get advice or ask for feedback but eventually make the decision by ourselves. The worst are decision makers who make up their mind and then consult just for the perception that the decision was made collaboratively. People are smart. They will figure out that we command, but pretend to consult. If you have already made up your mind, then announce the decision and take accountability for the results.

Vote

Voting decision-making is when an agreed percentage is the threshold for a decision to be accepted. Decision making by voting does not guarantee a good decision. It reflects popularity rather than thorough critique, comprehensive assessment and methodical evaluation. Every percentage between 50-75% still leaves us with a significant group that lost the vote and is not necessarily committed to the decision. Voting is a good indicator for how far we're from reaching across the board to commitment and how much more Dialogue is needed.

Consensus

Consensus decision-making is when everyone comes to agreement and fully supports the final decision. It is the most time consuming, exhausting, and lengthy decision-making process. Through this process original proposals are amended and compromised to address the concerns of the participants in the decision process. It is the process that promises the highest commitments of the team members. But it can be easily manipulated if the Dialogue rules are not followed carefully: Keep it safe and ask for every member's opinion if they don't speak out. Consensus is not achieved in silence. It is achieved in vocal conversations. It is achieved in fierce confrontations.

These four decision-making options represent increasing degrees of involvement, which result in increasing degrees of commitment. Of course we pay for it with decreasing degrees of efficiency.

What should be the preferred decision making process?

It depends on the situation. The more critical the speed of execution is, the more you will tend to reduce involvement of other people to achieve this prompt execution. The commitment is not there yet. Results may be poor. Sometimes instant actions are required. Sometimes you have to get things done promptly and without hesitation- usually during a crisis. If you explain carefully the reasons for the rush, you may even get commitment.

The complexity, width and depth of the subject also matters. The more complicated the execution is and the more resources it requires, a consensus decision-making process will provide a better accountability platform for the execution.

When you have more time, you should prioritize effectiveness over efficiency. Although the decision process will be lengthy and more people will be involved - the chances of successful implementation are very high. The extra time and effort by all involved to Dialogue thoroughly up front will save time, money and the stress of fixing mistakes later. Everyone contributes - everyone benefits.

MANAGE YOUR PERCEPTION

The male lion isn't the smartest animal in the jungle. Apes, Elephants and Parrots are more intelligent. The King of Beasts is neither the largest animal nor the largest cat. The tiger is. He isn't the fastest animal or even the fastest cat. The cheetah is. He isn't even the hunter among his own pride. It's the female lions that track and subdue prey.

Then, why is the lion considered the King of the jungle? It is because he has an impressive mane and a big roar.

This doesn't mean the lion is a fraud. If called upon, he can back up that roar. However, what makes the lion special is the combination of genuine power and behavior that effectively communicates that power to the world.

If we want to be lions – that is to say, the "kings and the queens" of our own profession – we need to adopt the same approach. Those of us who are on the path to corporate leadership should spend time perfecting the types of communication skills that generate respect and influence others.

People reach highly influential positions because they understand the power of perception and know how to leverage it. They use these skills to establish how they are perceived by others and to manage their reputation throughout the organization, stakeholders and the public.

A few years back, perception management was the lowest priority on my list. "Actions speak louder than words," people often heard me say. 'Reality shapes perceptions,' I thought naively. I have since changed my mind.

The way we are perceived is the reality in the eyes of our colleagues, friends, and managers and definitely in the media. Abraham Lincoln said, "Public sentiment is everything. With it, nothing can fail; without it, nothing can succeed."

The biggest potential mistake is confusing perception with manipulation. You will achieve nothing by manipulating others to follow your ideas, beliefs, or vision. Once you shift from being someone who influences through manipulation to being someone who influences through persuasion, you can't lose.

To ensure the respect of your peers, employees, bosses and eventually the general public, you can use the power of branding to further your professional and personal goals. How do you improve the way you are perceived by others? How do you build a strong personal brand?

First, you identify changes in attitude, behavior and character that will strengthen your brand. Then you commit to them. For example, this book is a commitment to change. Writing my commitments and sharing them with the public, reinforces my behaviors.

Second, you assess how you are perceived by others. Feedback gathering can be a painful task, especially if you are sincere about receiving honest criticism from your peers, bosses and employees. The self-assessment and feedback gathering is worthless if you are not making adjustments along the way.

Third, you discover your personal power by focusing on building credibility. Let people understand who you really are. Let them figure out that you have changed and that you are different. You should not shy away from your new brand.

Fourth, you may become the living embodiment of your new brand quickly (or not), but it will take time for others to notice, especially if a shift in perception is required. The process takes time so don't be discourage if results aren't immediate.

Fifth, you grow as you go. Keep what works and revise what doesn't. The most important part is to enjoy the journey. Good things will happen when you stick to your commitment to yourself, regardless of the time it takes. The consequences of your actions, behaviors and decisions will empower you to reach your goals like never before.

Most importantly, you must be genuine with your intentions and maintain a congruence of your image brand with your true self. If gaps exist between what you want to be and who you really are, you need to work to align the two. Otherwise perception management isn't real, it's only a facade.

DEVELOP INFLUENTIAL COMPETENCE

Martin Orlov, the new CIO of a Fortune 500 retail company, was in a very tough situation. The company spent 10% of the overall expenditures year after year on the company's legacy IT system. The company's new ambition to expand the business into online retail would double the budget. The IT team believed in the legacy system they have been utilizing for more than 15 years. They did not attempt to replace it with a new platform.

Martin was confident that the legacy system could not be transformed into an ecommerce platform with mobile capabilities, social integration and global localized versions. During his first month he formed a committee comprised of the company's senior management and business unit managers to propose a plan for the required ecommerce expansion while decreasing the technology expenditures.

Martin knew that the only way to reduce costs while enabling a new ecommerce technology was to eliminate the legacy system and move all the various platforms to an integrated one. The problem was that this proposal would increase the short-term capital investment, but pretty quickly the company would see additional revenue from online sales and over the long term, the company would see a drop in operational expenses.

Martin knew that this plan would step on the toes of many executives that would be affected. Most of them treated the legacy platform like it was their baby. He neither had the power to force any of them to accept his plan nor did he have rapport with the business unit managers. He did not know them well enough and they did not know him either.

However, Martin was not a person who would be easily discouraged by a challenge. He knew the problem before he joined the company but was determined to make a difference.

Martin started meeting with all the system's programmers and analysts. He shared his ideas, found points of resentment and provided solutions to objections. When he reached an agreement, he asked for a sign-off on the proposal. When he faced resentments, he moved the people who objected to the bottom of the list and decided to address them later on, when he would be ready with more supporters.

The process was exhausting and time consuming but Martin was dedicated to receiving full support through one-on-one meetings. He avoided "herd" meetings where some people tend to follow other people because of politics or reporting lines. Martin scheduled second and third meetings with people who had objections and showed them the wide support he had received on the signed-off document, using the power of social acceptance to support the plan.

Martin expected to complete this process in one month, but it took two months to be able to present it to the committee. The committee members were surprised when the presentation was done by the Vice President of Technology, who was previously the most vocal supporter of the legacy platform.

The plan was approved on the first committee meeting because Martin addressed all objections and made sure that all resentments were brought to the table, and discussed and documented.

After this success most of us would probably take it immediately to the Executive Committee or even to the Board. Right?

Not Martin.

Martin repeated the same process with higher management. He met them one-on-one, explained the plan, showed the signed-off documents and added more supporters at the top management. He left objections to be addressed again in second and third rounds of personal meetings. This process was faster because the top management did not deal with the technical details so much, rather they focused more on the business impact and the cost.

Martin customized every presentation to the specific needs of the people he met. He ended up with more than ten presentation versions, but those versions were varied to address the specific goals of stakeholders from their point of view.

The Executive Committee, who included all C-Level executives and some board members, resolved to implement the plan and bring it for a Board approval.

After this success most of us would probably take it immediately to the Board. Right?

Not Martin.

Martin met every Board member one-on-one and eventually ended up meeting some of their advisors to ensure that they were not influenced by informal stakeholders. Powerful advisors, even though they are not part of the Board or the executive team, still have a strong circle of influence.

Martin even asked for the Chairman's support before the Board meeting. The Chairman was very influential with the public directors. Martin had seen supportive directors change their mind too many times without shame on the spot and reverse their support just to follow their political cycle of influence. There was too much at stake to let it happen this time. Martin wanted to avoid surprises because failure would mean the end of his short tenure with the company.

Two more weeks of personal meetings and calls with the Board of Directors resulted in full support. The Board resolved to eliminate the legacy system and invest $3 million in an integrated ecommerce platform, which ultimately would have lower operational costs. Within three months of joining the company, Martin had achieved the impossible.

Influential Competence is the single most important skill that will take you to the top. It is the ability to influence peers and top management to undertake crucial decisions.

Martin's tough situation is a common one for new and experienced leaders. Most decisions are made collaboratively by committees, boards and teams. The informal decision making process is more powerful than the formal decision making process.

How can you develop Influential Competence? To answer this question, let's look again at the methods Martin used to convince his peers to take on tough and potentially divisive challenges and solve them through consensus.

Informal power

Identify all stakeholders and make sure that they support the plans. It is surprising how many informal circles of influence exist within an organization. Some call it politics and decide to rise above the game. Ignoring the game guarantees failure. The informal stakeholders are, in most organizations, more powerful than the formal decision makers.

One –On-One

Large meetings should be held to seal decisions, not reach them. Meetings are proven to be the toughest platform to make decisions on controversial issues, innovative strategies, disruptive technologies or turning points. You can never be sure of the various support groups that have been formed over years. The most time consuming but most effective way to dissolve objections or controversy is the one-on-one meeting. In this way you can customize your presentation to the point of view of your audience. Rushing to bring a decision to the group is exciting, but it is not an effective process.

Personal Agendas

Check your personal agenda at the door but check out the personal agenda of the person you want to influence. Everyone has a personal agenda. Revealing personal agendas benefits the persuasion process. Personal agendas are not necessarily negative. They are directions that people and their teams have already engaged with or are committed to. Personal agendas might also be out of the scope of the business as well. Whether personal agendas are legitimate or not, the more you reveal the better we can handle objections. This process requires trust and good relationships to remove the barriers of sharing personal information. Understanding what drives people and showing them "what's in it for them," is still a powerful influential interaction.

Influential Competence is not something we were born with. It can be developed by following the process of identifying the formal and informal stake holders from all corporate hierarchies and outside the corporation, meeting them one-on-one as many times as needed to handle objections and by addressing the stake holders' personal agendas without pushing your own personal agenda.

TAKE A STAND

Ben presented the project very professionally. He clearly covered the scope of the project and the outline of the various tasks. He explained the reasons it was behind schedule, and discussed three ways to get it back on track. At the end of his presentation I asked, "So which of the three options are you recommending?" He replied that this was for the Board of Directors to decide.

"After all," he said, "They have the authority to decide. Not me." It struck me that this person, a senior manager, did not want to take a stand.

"You are the expert," I said, "It is up to you to recommend, to influence and to persuade others about what you believe is the best option for the company."

As a leader it is important to have a strong point of view. Raising a huge banner is better than waving a little flag like everyone else. Most people do not rise above the crowd to set out strong principles. To be a leader means you are willing to take a stand and hold on to your principles, no matter what.

Good leaders take a stand on issues if the consequences are not in their favor. It is easy to take a stand on a non-controversial issue, but what about the more controversial issues? What about taking a strong stand against a trend, group, or even management? Taking a stand against a policy, a way of doing business or a common behavior, is the riskiest thing a leader can do. And yet it is the most powerful way to make your impact on the world.

So what if somebody says, "Don't fight a lost war?" Should you fight against all odds? Should you take the risk? It depends on how closely the issue at stake matches your core values and beliefs. It is a very personal decision. The smaller the gap, the more I will fight for my stand. What about you?

Of course, good leaders know when to make compromises for the good of the group. Being a contrarian just for the sake of being contrarian won't get you anywhere. Your stand should be congruent with your core values, your personality and what you believe to be the right thing for your organization, given the information you have.

Leadership is about finding the courage to take a stand on important matters and controversial issues. Leaders are brave. They do not compromise on what they believe to be the right thing to do. As the saying goes: "You've got to stand for something…or you'll fall for anything."

PERSUADE IN THE BOARDROOM

It was a long meeting, much longer than the allotted time. The discussion had evolved into confrontation. We ended up at a dead-end, incapable of making a decision.

It started after presenting a proposal that received strong objections. I exhausted every possible justification in an effort to convince the team to support the proposal. More pushing was met with more resistance. We ended the debate with a decision to come back to it later. In other words... procrastination.

We face these situations day in and day out, don't we? It is an art more than a science to win a confrontation. Right?

Wrong.

The problem is not about the "art." Trying to "win" doesn't work. Mutual resolution is important, even if the resolution does not fit our game plan. Easier said than done.

Confrontations happen and unexpected objections occur. Can you avoid these kinds of obstacles? No. Expect them.

"Be Prepared."

That's the motto of the Boy Scouts.

"Be prepared for what?" Someone once asked Lord Baden-Powell, the founder of the Boy Scouts.

"Be prepared for anything," was his reply.

No wonder Boy Scouts become good leaders—they are prepared.

I was not prepared for objections. However, when no alternative solutions were presented, the manipulations began. At this junction, it is often easier to start manipulating rather than to persuade. After all, the win is important. We can easily drift into dictating our way to make a decision, which will probably result in lousy execution, rather than working our way to a meaningful win-win outcome.

Commanding or dictating your way toward a resolution may work in few situations (for example, in a time limited crisis or military battle). A smart military officer used to commanding on the battlefield will eventually mix his decision making process with consensus management. Eventually, he will become a General.

This is called Situational Leadership.

Situational Leadership was developed by Paul Hersey, professor and author of the book *Situational Leader*, and Ken Blanchard, leadership guru and author of *The One Minute Manager*.

The fundamental underpinning of Situational Leadership is that there is no "best" style of leadership. Effective leadership is task-relevant. The most successful leaders are those that adapt their leadership style to the majority of the group they lead (or influence) and to the task that needs to be accomplished.

Decision "commanding" does not work in the boardroom. You have to make your way to the hearts of the people whom you want to influence, aligning your persuasion methods to the situation. It is beyond what people say. It is about how people feel. For example, someone may object to a proposal because they are a "do it right" person (regardless of the circumstances) while the proposer is a "do it now" person, who needs a solution quickly even if it is not 100% right. Confrontation guaranteed.

You have to look out for the underwater currents in order to avoid drifting into unwanted directions. Thorough preparation is required. So is commitment to learning the various personalities of the people you work with and the determination to develop a relationship with them.

You grow into leadership by developing your persuasion skills. Persuasion rather than dictation makes things happen.

ACHIEVE CLARITY

Michael's face turned as red as a tomato when he gasped, "What do you mean 'recall the product'?"

"The FDA instructed us to stop selling the supplement because it has to get FDA approval," Marissa replied, squirming in her chair.

"How come?" Michael banged on the desk. "We decided to launch it in Asia first. Why did you launch it in the US?"

"No Michael," Marissa replied unconvincingly. "You were in the meeting when we decided to take a risk and launch it in the US."

"Are you kidding?" Michael's voice increased. "I wouldn't even think about making such a ridiculous mistake."

Marissa, the Chief Marketing Officer, decided she was better off recruiting some help from her colleagues.

"Check it with the rest of the team before jumping to conclusions," Marissa replied, knowing that finger pointing wouldn't change the facts. They had screwed up. She decided to focus on rectifying the mistake first and pacifying her CEO later.

Almost three hours later, the executives gathered in the boardroom. The product had been removed from the website but the boardroom was just as tense as ever.

"We had three serious failures this year," Michael began.

"Michael, we don't have clarity about decisions that we make," said Beth, the COO. "We leave meetings with different ideas of what decisions were made. There is no clarity of what we should focus on most. This product launch went under the radar for all of us because it was not coordinated well."

Silence filled the room. Michael frowned while he thought of a response.

Have you ever left meetings "thinking" that you knew what had been decided, only to find out later that you were wrong?

It happens to all of us, but there is a way to avoid this.

Define a Thematic Goal

There are long-term strategic goals and short-term objectives. A Thematic Goal bridges between the gap between short-term objectives and the long-term goals.

I love Patrick Lencioni's definition of a Thematic Goal as: "A single, qualitative focus or rallying cry that is shared by the entire leadership team and ultimately, by the entire organization-and that applies for only a specified period of time." The Thematic Goal is the top priority of the entire leadership team for a given period of time. It aligns employees throughout the organization and is a tool for resetting direction when things get out of sync.

Thematic Goals are powerful because of the process that goes into setting them. The leadership team members provide their suggestions, discuss the priorities and decide on the single most important goal that will be shared collectively. It requires every member to commit to the same goal and assume collective accountability to achieving it.

Is it possible to reach consensus before making crucial decisions? What if one or two members do not agree?

Well, it depends on if they share their disagreements or keep quiet. Working in Asia for the last 12 years has taught me to mine and dig deep for disagreements. Too many times projects fail because leaders wrongly assume that their teams are on board. Every time you make a decision, you should ask each person one by one for agreement and commitment. If even one person disagrees, their concerns must be heard thoroughly. The dissenters must feel that they have been heard well and their concerns have been considered.

CONSENSUS OF COMMITMENT

You can achieve Consensus of Commitment, even without reaching Consensus of Agreement, by carefully listening and considering the thoughts of others and by allowing enough time to argue, discuss and convince them. This can be performed through a process known in Intel's culture as "disagree and commit."

Disagree and commit is a very powerful concept. It is a validation of a different opinion, a commitment to move forward, and most importantly, a dedication to get things done. Plans are implemented. Strategy is executed.

Communication of Decisions

Unfortunately leadership teams that successfully commit to Thematic Goals still fail to execute because of one common mistake. They fail to communicate the decisions across the organization – up, down and sideways.

We usually focus on cascading decisions down to our team members but often ignore other stakeholders, such as board members.

Peer-to-Peer Accountability

Once we commit to a Thematic Goal it is the responsibility of everyone to call upon any of their peers who don't meet their commitments. Most people don't confront their peers when they fail to meet their commitments as they think it's their peer's boss' job to call upon their peer commitments.

It's not.

Peer to peer accountability is very powerful when it becomes part of an organization's culture. People start taking their commitments seriously when they are called out by their friends. They try much harder when they feel that they risk relationships by disappointing their colleagues.

Reaching clarity in decision-making is not difficult. Just follow the process. Define a Thematic Goal. Listen, consider and discuss objections openly. Reach Consensus of Commitment by asking dissenters to "disagree but commit." Then cascade the decision across all levels of the organization, holding people accountable to their commitments.

DISCERN BEFORE YOU DECIDE

We wake up every morning to a new day of challenges. Some are minor issues that can be resolved by others. Some are important matters that require our utmost attention.

Minor issues have short-term and non-recurring impacts. Major issues have long-term repetitive impacts. The former don't really make a difference in our lives. The latter does make a significant difference and therefore requires our immediate and focused consideration.

For example, let's take a $5,000 dollar business expense. A business trip that costs $5,000 is a minor matter because it is a one-time expense. Yet, for a new employee with a $5,000 monthly salary, it is a major matter because it is a long-term recurring cost, which over 10 years will accumulate to more than a $1 million.

Purchasing a single $1,000 dress is just a one-time expense but a $1,000 monthly mortgage will cost us $300,000 over 25 years.

Mistakes we make in small matters don't make a significant impact on our lives, right? Yet, blunders on some matters can turn our lives upside-down. Marry the wrong person and your life is miserable for years. Choose a profession which doesn't make you happy and you end up unhappy for years. Select the wrong business partner and you risk a successful business. These decisions are life changing. They take us on completely different life journeys. Good or bad.

People who lack discernment are seldom in the right place at the right time in their life journey.

Some people appear to always be lucky. It's more likely that these people create their own "luck" by being discerning about what is most important.

Discernment is determination of the value of a certain matter or event. We are going past mere perceptions, to make judgments about the matter or the event.

A discerning individual possesses wisdom and has good judgment; especially with regard to matters often overlooked by others. Discernment is crucial for leadership success and nobody ever seems to talk about it.

Here is a 4-step blueprint for moving toward becoming a discerning leader:

1. Switch from the lower brain to the upper brain

Our brain has three layers, which have evolved over millions of years. These layers interconnect but actually act independently and are often at war with one another.

The lower "reptilian" or primitive brain is the "fight-or-flight" part. It is all about acting and reacting without a lot of thinking. This is the brain that causes us to respond immediately to danger.

The middle "mammalian" brain is the place of our emotions. It's where strong feeling such as love, joy, sadness, anger and jealousy arise.

The upper "primate" or logical brain is the place of rational decision-making. This brain collects data, analyzes it and makes practical decisions.

You don't want to make decisions when your primitive brain is in control nor when your emotional brain is in charge. These two are responsible for a state of mind that might not be right for the issue at hand. How do you move to the logical brain? Just….STOP. Detach from the situation and wait until you are back to the rational, logical, and lucid zone.

2. Distinguish facts from assumptions

Many times, we rush decisions based on assumptions rather than facts. We have so many perceptions which are accepted as truth while in reality they are based on assumptions. Assumptions and perceptions create false reality. You have to be free of this dangerous state of mind.

You are capable of making smart decisions based on facts if you take the time to switch from the primitive and emotional brain to the logical brain. It is impossible to look at facts and eliminate assumptions when you are in an emotional state of mind.

3. Find the root of the matter

Every day we solve problems only to find that we face the same problems over and over again.

Why?

Because we rarely take time to think, 'What was the root-cause for this issue? What could be done differently to stop the problem from re-occurring? or what's the one reason that things happen the way they happen over and over again?'

4. Listen to your gut

How many times has your intuition "spoken" to you and been correct?

How many times have you not listened?

Listening to your gut is not guesswork. It requires silent reflection. It requires contemplative vigilance. It requires asking introspective questions. You must trust that the answer will reveal itself when the time is right. It is important to hold off making up your mind until the truth emerges.

Above all, you want to be alert to the signs placed in your path and follow them with vision, intuition and an open mind. Being blind to your insights might be even more restrictive than being physically blind.

Try the 4-step blueprint to becoming more discerning in your work and life. After all, a single wrong decision can change the course of your entire life.

ACTION

HIRE YOUR REPLACEMENT

A while ago I called Marvin and suggested he start looking for his replacement. "Aren't you happy with my performance?" asked Marvin. "Do you plan to fire me?" I could hear the worry in his voice.

"Not at all," I replied. "I want to promote you. How can you be promoted if you have not groomed your replacement?"

Who is your successor? If you don't have one, you have probably been in the same position for too long. Your chances of getting a promotion are better if you have a successor.

How strong should your successor be? The answer is that he or she should be stronger than you!

It is a tough dilemma. Isn't it? After all, it's human nature to be afraid of a successful, professional, highly skilled and competent successor who may put us in his or her shadow or pass us up altogether.

When you grow into a management position, you are no longer an individual professional who is only as good as your technical skills. Leaders

149

are only as good as their teams. The stronger the team, the more successful the leaders.

If you dare to groom a better and stronger successor, it will reflect positively upon you. You will be perceived as confident, successful and brave. A sharp successor will push you out of your comfort zone. He or she will challenge you and reinforce your personal growth.

Years ago, as the Financial Controller of an American listed company, my technical skills were below the benchmark. My adaptive skills compensated for my technical skills. One day, I was interviewing candidates for the position of Accounting Manager. Amar was my first choice. He was a confidant and energetic CPA from a Big Four firm with superior technical, commercial and management skills. I hesitated. This guy was better than me, especially considering his youth and work experience.

I hired Amar and my job changed overnight. He took over the group accounting. He interacted professionally with our holding company, managed his team well and worked with me on innovative projects. I had a real trailblazer on my team. I never felt threatened even though I knew, as well as everybody else, that Amar was better at the job than me. Our team performance was incredible. In a year we did a corporate split, merger and acquisition. The Chairman and the CEO told me that he felt very comfortable in these endeavors because of the strong finance team. Shortly afterwards, I was promoted to CFO. Amar replaced me as the Financial Controller. A year later, I left the company for an international assignment and Amar replaced me as the CFO. It was a wonderful feeling to leave the legacy of a strong and capable successor. It was not then nor will it be the last time I groom my replacement. It is a proven way to scale the corporate pinnacle.

Who is your successor?

GET YOUR HANDS ON

It was a total failure. No doubt about it. It was one which I don't like to remember. I should, though. I want to share it with you so you will avoid such embarrassment in the future.

So what was this massive failure of mine? Was it a failure of a new strategic plan? Was it a Merger or Acquisition that ended without results? Was it a loss of a large customer contract?

Not at all!

It was a failure to simply follow up on a process. It was a failure to make sure that the one who was delegated a task was actually doing it. This issue wasn't the highest on my priority list, but it was the highest on my clients' priority list. It made my list completely irrelevant.

Konosuke Matsushita, who founded Matsushita said, "Big things and little things are my job. Middle level arrangements can be delegated." Leaders cannot delegate management. In the corporate world, leadership is well practiced management. Well practiced management is primarily getting things done.

Mary Parker Follett said in the 1920s that, "Managers get things done largely through other people - those in the unit who formally report to them as well as others around it who do not."

Is that right?

Henry Mintzberg is a Professor of Management Studies at McGill University in Montreal and the winner of numerous awards. He is the author of 15 books, including *Managers Not MBAs* and *The Rise and Fall of Strategic Planning*. In his latest book, *Managing*, Mintzberg presents a new model of managing that puts the manager between the unit he or she has formal responsibility for and its surroundings: the rest of the organization and the outside world relevant to the business unit (customers, vendors, etc.).

Managing takes place in three dimensions: through information, people and direct action.

Managing Through Information

We process information to encourage other people to take action. On the information dimension, we communicate (all around) and control (inside).

We promote the flow of information all around and use it to drive behavior within our department (controlling). Here we are two steps away from the real action.

Managing With People

When we manage with people we move one step closer to the action. On this dimension we help people make things happen. They are the doers. We lead people within the business unit and link people outside it.

Managing Action Directly

When we manage action directly we are the doers. We get close to the action and we "just do it" rather than "get it done." In this case, we are not passive. This is not about sitting in the office and giving orders or making judgment on those actions. Nor it is about designing strategies, structures and systems to drive other people. We get personally involved in those actions, 'hands-on'.

We cannot be either information-oriented, people-oriented or action-oriented managers. We have to be all of them in order to be well-rounded managers. This balance is essential to success. Whenever one dimension takes over, we face organizational failures.

There is one kind of management that does not work: Email management. Too many of us depend on emails to manage people both inside and outside our business units. Emails are limited to the poverty of words alone. You cannot hear the tone of voice, see the gestures and body language or feel the presence. You cannot support emotional, delicate and complex interactions. Managing is as much about all these things as it is about the content of the messages.

As much as micro-management has a negative impact, macro-management is worse. Managers who are disconnected don't know what's going on. "Hands-off" too often amounts to "brains-off." So, be a well-rounded manager. Play in all dimensions and make sure to be "hands-on" and "brains-on."

EXECUTE TO TURN GOALS INTO RESULTS

In the mid-1990's a friend told Jack Welch, the CEO of General Electric, about a new methodology for making a quantum increase in inventory turns in manufacturing operations. GE could generate cash if it could increase its inventory turnover. The leading practitioner of this idea was American Standard, which had achieved 40 inventory turns compared to the average of four at most companies.

Welch didn't just try to get the concept or send his people to investigate. He made the trip personally to meet American Standard employees and learn the process of how to overcome resistance in implementing the new methodology.

By involving himself both personally and deeply with the subject, Welch was able to get the necessary changes rolling quickly at GE. Jack Welch was a leader that made execution his highest priority.

Execution is the major job of a business leader. It is a discipline that happens through personal involvement. It's a systematic process of: rigorously discussing the "hows" and "what-ifs," tenaciously following-up and ensuring accountability. It's not enough to make your mark as a high-level thinker who is not interested or involved in the "how" of getting things done. As a leader, your job is to transform the vision into measurable tasks, to involve people in the shaping of the strategic plan, to set milestones for progress and to put contingency plans in place for unexpected issues.

Unfiltered Information

The major challenge we face today is that by the time information reaches us it has been filtered into reports designed to present others' perceptions and agendas. The higher we are in the corporate ladder, the more filtered the information we receive is. The more filtered information that we use, the further we are from reality.

We must insist on realism. Many organizations are full of people who try to avoid reality. Reality is uncomfortable and often reveals mistakes. Realism is at the heart of execution. Make it a priority.

To get in touch with reality through direct access to data, you need to bypass the corporate data gatekeepers, perception managers, "gut feeling" wizards and other information manipulators. If you are an aspiring leader, using "hands on" information will reward you consistently. Business Intelligence Tools crunch mountains of data in seconds and organize it into simple information. I have been asked, many times, "Why do your waste your time crunching data when you have staff to do it?"

My reply?

"The reality is viewed differently through different glasses." Note that analyzing the raw data for yourself is especially important when a critical decision has to be made or when you feel the information you have received has been filtered, manipulated or analyzed subjectively (which is often the case!).

Follow Through and Follow-Up

"New age" leadership advisors suggest that you set up goals and objectives and follow-up after execution. Been there, done that. It did not work well. Each stage of execution faces challenges. If challenges are not identified as they occur and appear only at follow up, it's too late. Deadlines are missed, dependent projects are slowed and costs begin to skyrocket.

Don't follow-up after. Instead, follow through during. Teams need guidance throughout the execution process. Many challenges are overcome through collaboration. You can address conflicts that stand in the way and resolve them before it is too late.

Create mechanisms for following through, such as status meetings, task lists, clear ownership of tasks and timetables. Smaller tasks are better than bigger tasks. Simple tasks are easier than complicated ones.

Execution is KEY to success. Get your hands on unfiltered information and implement follow-through and follow-up mechanisms to turn goals into results.

EMBRACE ACCOUNTABILITY

"How did that happen?"

How many times have you heard yourself asking this? Missed targets, lost sales, failed projects, you name it. At the end of the day, we hold people accountable for the expectations we have of them. Your major challenge in keeping people accountable is twofold: how to set expectations and how to deal with unmet expectations.

Roger Connors and Tom Smith are recognized around the world for their Accountability Training. They are the authors of four books about accountability, among them, *How Did That Happen?* Connors and Smith define accountability as, "A personal choice to rise above one's circumstances and demonstrate the ownership necessary for achieving desired results –to See It, Own It, Solve It and Do It." They claim that to hold someone accountable means, "To effectively form, communicate, align and inspect the fulfillment of an expectation in the positive, principled way that enables people to achieve results now and in the future."

Accountability is easier to achieve when you accept three fundamental beliefs. First, people don't fail to follow through because there is something wrong with them. If you do not believe in your people, you can do little or nothing to force change except by punishing them. Second, people are doing their best to fulfill your expectations. They want things to work as much as you do. Third, when things go wrong, there is something wrong with what "you" as participant and leader are doing. When I believe that I am part of the problem, I take control of future outcomes and internalize the continuous need to improve my effectiveness rather than looking for faults in others.

When you fail to place accountability where it belongs, you face severe consequences. Everyone is busy pointing fingers at everyone else, deadlines aren't met and the work remains below standard. Things won't get better until people stop trying to blame each other and start addressing the issue that caused the problem in the first place. This cycle will continue until everyone takes accountability for their contribution to the problem and focuses on seeking solutions.

What happens when a poor performer "drops the ball" and isn't held accountable for the results? Usually, the assignment is given to someone you feel you can count on. Asking top performers to pick up the pieces will eventually wear them out. They will feel that their heavier workload is punishment for good performance. Taking a poorly executed assignment away from someone just reinforces poor performance. The message is, "Don't worry if you screw up. Someone else will fix it." For unmotivated employees, less work is a reward for poor performance.

Failing to hold others accountable creates the perception that you don't treat people fairly and equally. Pretty soon others on the team get the message about "what it takes to succeed around here" and the extent to which they can count on you as a leader.

Set Expectations

You cannot hold someone accountable if you haven't set clear expectations. You will get better results by setting high expectations with the people involved in making it happen. In the complex business world, most expectations cannot be met by a single individual. Most complex tasks require a few individuals to set expectations for each task, regardless of their departments, job descriptions, and managers.

We all have a boss – someone who has expectations of us. Even a CEO has a boss. The Board of Directors has a boss – the shareholders they represent. Someone defines what is expected of all of us. We form links to others based on what is expected from us. Others ask us to join in their efforts to deliver what is expected of them. Eventually, we participate in "Expectation Teams" – some which we ourselves have formed and some that have been formed by others.

Communicate Expectations

It is obvious that you have to define the specifics of what you want to happen, who will make it happen and when it will happen. Communicating the "what" "when" and "who" without communicating the "why" will hardly engage people's minds. Definitely not their hearts. You need to address the "whys" differently to different people. Why is this important? Why me and not someone else? Why now? Why do it this way? Why would I want to do this? The best way to inspire people is to craft a compelling story that captures the imagination. You want people to buy into the cause.

Align Expectations

We align with our Expectation Team when they believe in the goal and commit themselves to deliver. Expectation alignment uplifts people in a way that engages their minds and hearts. It's an ignition reaction. Alignment with one or two people will spread the energy to the rest of the team. You cannot require people to buy- in enthusiastically and to bring their best of themselves. You can only persuade them.

But what if you fail to persuade? You are in a position to ask for compliance, right? Sure you are. But compliance doesn't deliver expectations the same way a buy-in does. People will move with you, not because they agree with your direction, but because they have decided that complying will satisfy their own interests.

Follow Up on Expectations

Follow-up meetings are opportunities to make sure everyone remains on the same page. They give you the chance to correct misalignment before things get out of control. You need to take advantage of follow-up meetings to facilitate solutions, coach and mentor people, help move things and make people successful.

Accountability Culture

Lack of accountability creates and reinforces a culture of blame, which, in turn, generates other problems. You may notice increased avoidance as well as a pervasive "don't get caught" attitude. Employees take fewer risks (or stop trying altogether) because no one wants to be blamed if something goes wrong. "Blamestorming" sessions thrive, creating a cycle of blame that ultimately shuts down communications.

Many times we have talented people who want to be part of a company that makes a difference in the world, but for some unknown reason, just don't deliver results. They are willing and they are able, but they either lack accountability or are operating in a culture that hurts their chances. What does the term culture mean in this scenario? It means: "The way we do things around here."

Connors and Smith write that a culture of accountability is a, "Place where people think and act, on a daily basis, in a manner necessary to develop successful solutions, find answers, overcome obstacles, triumph over any trouble that might come along and deliver results."

People in a culture of accountability make sure they do what they say they will do, commit themselves to getting to the truth, no matter what, and feel free to say what needs to be said.

Accountability is not something that happens when things go wrong. It is something that you continually embrace with every new task.

STOP MULTI-TASKING

There was a time when I envied super multi-tasking executives. The first impression I had was that they succeeded to outpace everyone else by juggling various tasks at the same time. They wrote emails while chairing meetings, text messages while they were talking, browsed the internet and completed calls before understanding the topic being discussed. It is only when you look at the quality of their work, the lack of details, the shallow ideas and the low attention to detail, that you start wondering whether these super multi-taskers achieve anything at all.

Can we really do multiple things at once and be more productive?

Studies show that multitasking is not as effective as concentrated tasks. These studies have indicated that people show deficits in performance when doing two very simple tasks at the same time. Our brain simply cannot focus on more than one basic task at once. For example, we can chew gum while we work, but cannot simultaneously focus on multiple complex tasks. Our brain must switch its attention from one thing to another. Every time we do this, our brain undergoes a process that takes time.

When it comes to paying attention, multi-tasking is a myth. The brain naturally focuses sequentially, one thing at a time. We are biologically incapable of processing rich attention inputs simultaneously.

John Medina explains in his book *Brain Rules* that when we attempt to complete many tasks at one time, or alternate rapidly between them, it takes longer to complete tasks and they are subject to errors. In the interim between each exchange, the brain makes no progress whatsoever and we lose time in the process. Although the brain is complex and can perform a myriad of tasks, it does not multi-task well.

Medina also shows that it takes 50% longer to accomplish a task when the person is interrupted. Not only that, he or she makes up to 50% more errors. Evidence about how bad we are at multi-tasking includes the performance of people who drive while talking on their cell phone. According to *Brain Rules*: "Cell phone talkers are a half second slower to hit the brakes in emergencies. In a half second a driver going 100 km per hour travels 20 meters. Only drunk drivers have more accidents than people talking on cell phones while driving!"

We often see people texting while engaged in a conversation. These texters will miss a great part of what is said. In addition, by not maintaining eye contact and paying complete attention to the conversation, the person who is busy texting conveys the impression that they aren't interested and do not care about what the other person thinks.

We don't have to be multitaskers to be high performers. We have to be extremely organized, meet deadlines, have a list of things we want to do and make sure they get done.

Here are some ideas on how to be more effective and more creative;

- Turn off the email alerts in our computers and cell phones. Also mute the text alerts (and emails) in our cell phones.
- Close the Internet browser windows you don't use, especially social media and communication applications such as Skype or Windows Live.
- Limit unscheduled colleague interruptions.
- Block time to check e-mails and block separate time for creative work, important projects and high-priority tasks. E-mails are like chocolate - they are irresistible, often of no real value, and there is no such thing as eating just one.

If you don't want to be like Pavlov's dog, responding to every interruption; if you don't want to look like a circus juggler, or if you want to be less stressed and more effective…stop trying to do a million things at once.

BE SUCCESSFUL IN UNCERTAIN WORLD

For most of us, the first 18 to 22 years of life were filled with relative certainty. In school, math problems had predictable solutions, which could be found at the end of the book or in the next day's lesson. Science experiments usually resulted in predictable outcomes. You could be fairly certain of what was going to happen next.

This treasured certainty abruptly ended as soon as we graduated from school, college or university. After 18-22 years of certainty and predictability, it was time to experience the exact opposite.

Business, work and life in general are not predictable...at all. Suddenly, we are suddenly required to make decisions without any certainty, predictability or even probability of the outcome. As a result, many of us freeze up in procrastination or end up making the wrong decisions in uncertain circumstances.

As a leader you don't have a choice. If you don't make decisions quickly, decisively and confidently, you will fail at tasks. You make most of your decisions without having all of the information required and without the ability to predict the outcome. Rupert Murdoch once said that great leaders make more than 20 important decisions every day and probably half of these decisions are wrong. This kind of uncertainty drives most people nuts, doesn't it?

This is true not only for your business and career, but also for your personal life. For example, in the western world the divorce rate has reached 50%. Uncertainty takes over every aspect of our lives in the 21st century. In order to be successful in the unpredictable circumstances of business, career and life, it is crucial that you are aware of uncertainty and that you develop strategies to cope with it.

Here is how you can become successful in an uncertain world. Let's use the business of stock trading to learn how to operate in complete uncertainty. The probability of making money in the stock market is 50% in the long term, because the stock market is a zero-sum game. This means that successful stock traders develop an edge to help turn the odds to their side. They are able to accomplish this feat because they run with their winners and cut their losses short. They are able to excel in a business with a 50% probability of success because they follow a few simple strategies. You too can adopt these six simple strategies into your business, career and personal life.

1. Decide With Incomplete Information

If you wait for all of the complete information before taking action, you may end up waiting forever. Many leaders become stuck in the 'analysis-paralysis' syndrome, where they continue searching for answers and analyzing possible outcomes while their competitors are already implementing. You can avoid the 'analysis-paralysis' syndrome by recognizing that your decision has been made based on incomplete information and by creating an actionable plan to mitigate the risks associated with it.

2. Act Quickly

The Perfect Moment doesn't exist. Waiting for the perfect moment is like waiting for the exact alignment of the stars. If you want to make a change, you have to be willing to do it right now. Not later. Not tomorrow. New Year's resolutions are an example of waiting for the perfect moment. Why should you wait for the beginning of a new year to make a resolution?

If there were such a thing as a perfect moment, we'd all be making perfect decisions every single time and no one would ever make a bad decision. The perfect moment is now. There is never a single right time. It is always the right time.

People that procrastinate are subject to the Law of Diminishing Intent, which says, "The longer you wait to do something you should do now, the greater the odds that you will never actually do it." Act quickly. Act now!

3. Look at the Downside

When you make decisions quickly using incomplete information, you increase the risk of failure. You need to assess the risks associated with your decision and ask "what if" the decision ends up being unsuccessful. It is quite obvious that most people make decisions without looking at the potential downsides. Don't make this mistake. Always be prepared in case things don't go well as expected.

4. Execute Flawlessly

An excellent execution of a mediocre decision reaps far better results than a poor execution of an excellent decision. Focus on the execution more than on the decision. Once you make a quick decision based on incomplete information ensure that your execution is no less than perfect. Poor execution in uncertain environment compounds the chances of failure.

5. Mitigate the Risk

Successful investors never decide to invest in anything without a clear exit strategy in place. Successful stock traders never take a trade without setting a 'Stop Order' in place first. They don't leave anything up to luck. They don't count on their ability to make the right decision quickly enough when the odds turn against them (which happens 50% of the time). They decide on a risk mitigation strategy BEFORE they take on the trade. You should do the same. Every uncertain decision you make should have a risk mitigation strategy in place before you make it.

You would expect that a 50% rate of divorce would encourage certain risk mitigation strategies, such as prenuptial agreements. But few people take such precautions. The problem is that prenuptial agreements often seem so utterly unromantic during the most romantic moments. But they can end up being so right if a marriage happens to end in a legal separation, a divorce or with a death. According to American Academy of Matrimonial Lawyers President Marlene Eskind Moses, only 3% of couples have prenuptial agreements.

In business we also tend to become romantic and fall in love with our decisions. When this happens we do not mitigate the risks before we make critical decisions. Don't make this mistake. Mitigate your risks in advance because when the odds turn against you (and they will at some point) it will be too late.

6. Cut Your Losses Short

You would be astonished by the number of people who have lost money in the stock market because instead of selling their plummeting stock and using that money to purchase climbing stocks, they held on, waiting for the original stock to rebound. Many leaders continue to hold on to losing projects that are a result of their own decisions rather than to divest, abolish or abort in order to cut their loses short. The key is to detach yourself emotionally from the wrong decisions you have made.

These are the six simple strategies that will make you successful in embracing uncertainty.

The 21st century is the century of uncertainty. Feel comfortable with uncertainty in order to become successful in your business, career and life. You will accomplish this if you decide with incomplete information, act quickly, look at the downside, executive flawlessly, mitigate the risks, and cut short your losses.

BE AN INTRAPRENEUR

I was standing the middle of the exhibition hall, in a state of astonishment. It was the last day of a five-day convention introducing brand new and innovative products. Participants were carrying bags of products that were just launched a few hours earlier. It was a meaningful moment for me and I was full of pride and a sense of fulfillment. I had spent the last two years attempting to reach this pivotal moment, and knew that there was even more challenges to overcome in the future. This was the moment when I realized what you could accomplish through intrapreneurship.

I have been passionate about health, wellness and well being for years and even pursued business opportunities as an entrepreneur in these markets before I became CEO. I was excited about the idea of continuing to pursue my dreams, passions and interests as an executive, even though I was not the owner.

"Would it be possible to pursue a personal interest which is outside of my employer's core business?" This was a question I asked myself three years ago. I was not sure of the answer. No other employees had done so to my knowledge. To do so would require guts. I would have to risk failure. It would require an investment of my personal time as well as the company's resources. It would also require an entrepreneurial spirit that most corporate executives usually do not pursue once they start working for other people and stop working for themselves. Do I have what it takes to achieve this goal?

When most corporate executives are asked for their ultimate dream, they reply, "I want to be my own boss." They want time and financial freedom, but very few actually ever achieve their dreams. They do not want to leave their comfort zone, take risks or they cannot afford the burden of financing their venture.

Do you want to feel unsatisfied, unfulfilled and wasted for the rest of your life? If not, you should adjust your focus from the ultimate goal to the journey itself. Once you switch your focus and intent from the ultimate goal and begin to focus on the journey, you can start to embrace new ideas of achieving your purpose wherever you are in the present moment. You do not need to quit your job. You do not need to take new financial risks like debt or loss of income. You just have to change the way you think. You will get all the rewards of entrepreneurship once you shift the focus from the ultimate results to the journey itself.

This kind of entrepreneurship has been termed as intrapreneurship. Intrapreneurship is the act of behaving like an entrepreneur while working for an organization. This way of thinking was what I needed to use to pursue my own interests and dreams while working for a corporation.

An Intrapreneur is an executive who works for a corporation and who takes direct responsibility for turning an idea into a profitable finished product. Intrapreneurship integrates risk-taking and innovative approaches that have been previously attributed to entrepreneurship.

In 1985, *TIME* Magazine published an article titled: "Here come the Intrapreneurs," which discussed the intrapreneurship spirit. *Newsweek* followed in the same year with an article that quoted Steve Jobs as saying, "The Macintosh team was what is commonly known as intrapreneurship; only a few years before the term was coined—a group of people going, in essence, back to the garage, but in a large company."

Intrapreneurship requires executives to initiate and innovate without being asked to do so. Intrapreneurs transform ideas into profitable ventures by tapping into their creativity, passions and interests, while operating within their organizations.

Intrapreneurship gives executives the opportunity to redesign their job scope, formally or informally, and behave like entrepreneurs, while using the resources, capabilities and security of their employer.

Corporations can leverage on intrapreneurship to shake up the status quo by injecting the dynamic characteristics of entrepreneurship, without exposing intrapreneurs to the risks or accountability associated with entrepreneurial failure.

Google allows their employees to spend up to 20% of their time pursuing projects of their choice. 3M encourages many projects within the company and gives certain freedoms to employees to create their own projects. Intel also has a tradition of implementing intrapreneurship.

While entrepreneurs start their ventures independently and bear either the full risk of their failure or the fruit of their success, intrapreneurs are not independent, not liable to bear losses and they are not responsible for raising capital.

Take the capital risk and independency aside, entrepreneurship and intrapreneurship are very similar. They both require innovation, creativity, the ability to look at things in novel ways, a capacity to take calculated risks and the attitude that failures are lessons. Intrapreneur and entrepreneurs are imaginative and relentlessly seek out opportunities to reinvent themselves.

What will it take for you to become the next Intrapreneur of your organization?

- Develop a vision and purpose that is related to your personal passions and interests.
- Build a professional-support network.
- Expand your professional world in order to lead cross-functional teams.
- Challenge the status quo.
- Persevere in the face of uncertainty or failure.

Intrapreneurs are the energy behind new ventures that enable large companies to continue innovating and embarking into new markets, products and services. Would Blackberry have been more competitive if they had intrapreneurs? Sure, they would.

Don't wait until your company allows you the chance to pursue intrapreneurship. Pursue it yourself. The more successful companies are, the more they fail to innovate. There is nothing that fails like success.

Intrapreneurship is your chance to achieve a meaningful and fulfilling career, with all of the rewards and none of the major financial risks. Make sure that you take full advantage of this new way of thinking. I know I'm glad that I did!

ESTABLISH RITUALS

You may have heard of Timothy Ferriss and his book, *The 4 Hour Workweek*. This book quickly became a *New York Times* and *Wall Street Journal* bestseller. *The 4 Hour Workweek* offers its readers a path to success using only four hours each week. The concept is centered around the idea that you should only work four hours each week on important things, while outsourcing the more tedious work to a Virtual Assistant. In theory, this plan offers a combination of financial freedom, semi-retirement and quality business advice.

Sounds like a dream come true, doesn't it?

Personally, I have yet to meet a person who has achieved significant success by working only four hours a week. Successful people actually work longer and harder than most of us. I doubt that even Ferriss lives the type of lifestyle he pitches in his book, as evidenced by a recent Tweet of his, "…Another late night of editing…" (Sept 11, 2012). Sure sounds like hard work to me!

After publishing *The 4 Hour Workweek,* Ferriss published another book. This one is titled, *The 4 Hour Body*. This 567 page books promises you the ability to get fit and in shape in just four hours per month!

I have yet to meet a person who has managed to get in shape by only working out four hours a month. Nevertheless, the guy sells a lot of four hour books.

In the real world, true success takes more than four hours of commitment per week or per month. Here is a powerful blueprint that will help you achieve physical, mental, intellectual, relational, social and spiritual success in the real world. This blueprint for success also requires four hours of your time, not per week or per month, but per day. It's the 4 Hour Success Ritual!

Why does this plan call for a 4 hour daily ritual?

This plan has you commit yourself to a daily ritual because rituals are extremely powerful. Rituals become ingrained in your daily life and therefore, they are hard to break. A good ritual is one that will stick with you every day. For example, look at the ritual of brushing your teeth every day. We all know that it is vital to keep our teeth clean to avoid cavities and painful trips to the dentist office. But this knowledge isn't the only reason why we brush our teeth 2 or 3 times a day. We also do so because it is a ritual- something that we are accustomed to each and every day of our lives.

If you can make something positive into a daily ritual, then you will be able to follow it through day after day. And sticking with something is how you become successful at it!

The 4 Hour Success Ritual is a holistic approach to body, mind and spirit. It covers your physical, mental, intellectual, relational, emotional, social and spiritual foundations. These rituals help you to grow and to become both a better and a more successful person.

The 4 Hour Success Ritual consists of:

- One hour of Exercise for your path to physical health.
- One hour of Discernment for your path to mental, spiritual and emotional growth.
- One hour of Learning for your path to intellectual growth.
- One hour of Accomplishment for your path to execution, performance and achieving your plans.

The 4 Hour Success Ritual is the core reason behind my personal growth. It has truly changed my life. Let's get started understanding how these four rituals can work together to alter your life.

One Hour Exercise

You already know the vast benefits of physical exercise. You are aware of the importance of physical fitness when it comes to being able to enjoy your life to the fullest extent possible. But knowledge alone doesn't drive change- it takes motivation to force yourself to change your habits. It's the convictions that come from the heart, not from the head, that drive changes in behavior. Sure, pain, fear and sudden awareness of a medical problem could create this motivation for change, but by the time these motivators show up, it could be too late. Now is the time to drive change into your life!

The type of fitness regimen you choose is not important. You can choose to run, walk, bike, paddle, go to a fitness class, workout in the gym, ski, practice yoga or anything else. As long as you exercise, you will be improving the quality of your life!

The goal is to create a daily ritual of at least one hour of exercising. This daily ritual should be performed a minimum of four times per week, but the more you exercise, the better off you will be. You can alternate between aerobic exercises, strengthening exercises and flexibility exercises to achieve a complete workout each week. The daily hourly fitness regimen is a magical way to transform your body, improve your health, and boost your energy and to look and feel great!

One Hour Discernment

This hour is the single most important hour of your day. It will enable you to accomplish more in the remaining 23 hours of the day.

Discernment is not an easy process. It is something that takes both time and practice to master. Discernment is the ability to take a step back from your life and to judge the things that happen to you wisely and objectively. It is as though you are high above your life and looking down upon it from a different angle. Discernment allows you to assess situations from a different perspective.

If you're able to master discernment, then you're able to act objectively rather than emotionally. It allows you to find different answers from your usual perceptions. It helps you to step back and better understand why you and the people around you act the way that they do. Take time to reflect on your past and plan for your future. Make reflection and planning a part of your discernment process.

Reflection

Reflection is the foundation of your self-growth. The most practical way to improve yourself is to analyze what happened yesterday, reflect upon it today and determine what you can do better tomorrow.

Try using these 4 steps to effectively reflect upon your day:

1. What did I do well yesterday or today?
2. What did I do poorly?
3. What lessons did I learn?
4. What will I do differently next time?

Begin your reflections on a positive note. This helps to lift up your conscious and subconscious minds. It helps you to be more receptive and optimistic towards dealing with your constructive criticism.

If there is only one ritual that you take from the 4 Hour Success Ritual, it should be reflection. It will consistently improve your life by increasing your awareness of your own weaknesses and help you define the steps required to correct them. If you are able to reflect honestly about yourself, then awareness is the key to self-growth!

Planning

Review your life's purpose, vision and future plans. If you haven't defined your purpose, vision and plans for life, then you are driving down a road without a destination! This will eventually lead you nowhere. If however, you do have a purpose, a vision and goals, but you don't take the time to review them every day and embody them into your daily habits, then you are sitting in the backseat of your car as it drives you through life. The chances of reaching your destination from the backseat are very slim. Jump into the driver's seat, take control of your life and head towards your destination!

Planning helps you take control of your actions and will ensure that you actually reach your intended destination. If you are able to incorporate one small planning step per day through your daily rituals, over time these small steps will grow into giant steps. These giant steps will eventually help you to help you reach your goals.

One Hour Learning

You are probably thinking right now that you simply don't have enough time in your day to spend an hour learning. We all face this same challenge. Our lives are just too busy. But spending an hour learning each day will have tremendous effects on your intellectual growth, which will also have important benefits in the rest of your life.

There is an effective way to squeeze an hour of learning into your busy day. The way to accomplish this is to transform wasted time into learning time. Here are a few examples:

- Convert TV time into learning time
- Convert newspaper time into reading about self-growth time
- Keep a library in your restroom (Just in case you have a few minutes to learn something new!)
- Download informative audio books onto your MP3 players and listen as you commute
- Subscribe to a seminar or a workshop. If you don't have time to go you can sign up for virtual or online learning experiences
- Download educational material to your mobile device and read it whenever you have some spare time

Many of us spend more than one hour per day commuting to and from work. This is the perfect place to squeeze in some learning time. We also spend lots of time waiting in lines, standing around or waiting for other people. These are all times that we could be learning something new.

But simply reading, watching or listening to educational materials isn't enough for to covert what you consume into true knowledge. In order to truly convert this content into useable knowledge you must summarize it into your own words in order to internalize it. These summaries will become your internal reservoir of resources that you tap into whenever you need it. You can use it to aid in your own self-development and in the development of others.

One Hour Accomplishment

The first hour at the workplace is your Accomplishment Hour. This hour is dedicated to the execution of your dreams, ideas, plans and visions for the future. This is the hour of action!

While the other rituals can be performed in any order or at any time, it is best to perform the Accomplishment Hour first, as the first hour at your workplace. It should be done before anything else; before checking your e-mails, before answering calls and before others begin taking control of your schedule.

Block your Accomplishment Hour in your calendar as a recurring event every morning. My teammates know that this hour is my sacred time to move forward with my goals. This is the time that I work ON my business instead of working IN my business. This is the time that I invent, write, innovate and create new projects.

Only after the Accomplishment Hour are you ready to take on the day and read emails, make phone calls and work on other people's agendas. The more you grow as a leader, the more time you should allocate towards accomplishing your highest priorities. These priorities are driven by your life's purpose, vision and long-term goals. You don't find these priorities in your boss's task list or in your job description. This is the time where your heart and mind work coherently.

This is the personal plan that I follow. I don't do all of the 4 Success Rituals everyday. Not always. I skip workouts when I travel. I skip readings. I never skip discernment.

I don't necessarily spend four hours everyday. Most time I do, but occasionally I only spend one hour. Sometimes I spend six hours. Every now and then it is only 10 minutes. I don't keep the order every single time. The order of the 4 Hour Success Ritual is not important. What is important is developing a habit of doing it every day.

THE PINNACLE

We have scaled the pinnacle. We've traveled far together, rounding the fundamentals of Inner Leadership to become more intentional, expansive and effective. We are ready to advance our careers and lives after mastering Outer Leaderships foundations of dialogue, decision and action. Knowing and practicing these six practices will set you up to succeed in your career and even the biggest game of all – life.

The real gift is the journey you take as you strive to get better in your job and even better in your life. Enjoying the blessings of a great, meaningful, fulfilling and financially rewarding career requires hard work, struggle and commitment. The key success factor is never stop learning and never stop growing.

Allow yourself to live fully expressed without fear of what people will say behind your back. Push yourself every day to take new challenges in Inner Leadership and Outer Leadership. These challenges will energize you and inspire the people around you.

In the days ahead you will have moments that you will be on top of your game and make a significant difference in your business and in the lives of your employees, customers and family members. There will be days that strip you off your energy and motivation. That's life. Spend time reflecting on these different days and eventually, you will have more of the former days and less of the latter.

So what does the path ahead hold for you? Developing your Inner Leadership is the key to your success in the outer world of career and life. The more you will invest in your self development, the more you will see results in engagement of individuals and groups inside and outside your workplace. You will enjoy life and work. Work won't be just a way to make a living. You will live well while earning an income.

Don't forget to celebrate all of your successes, both big and small. Living the promise of this book will require much of you. You will stretch yourself to achieve your goals. You will soar above your shortcomings. You will challenge new summits. Stop from time to time to acknowledge and reward yourself. The world will celebrate your success too. It is your time now. Bring in everything you have learned. Dig deep to utilize your core strengths. Be your best. We will be there to witness your victory.

EPILOGUE

It was 9:00AM but it felt like more like 9:00PM. I ran the short distance from my hotel in Princeton, New Jersey to the parking lot dragging my suitcase behind me. It was raining so hard that by the time I got to the car, it looked like I had just jumped out of a swimming pool. Starting the engine, I left the parking lot behind me and headed towards Newark airport. The heavy showers limited the visibility to just a few meters ahead, making driving a tiresome task. As I crawled along in traffic I noticed how some of the other drivers were dealing with the situation. Looking around, I saw only gloomy faces. Nobody was smiling on this dark, cold and rainy morning.

The airport was not any better. Everyone was less polite than usual. All of the airport staff from security to immigration had woken up earlier to the same gloominess. I took a look at the flights board and was relieved to see that there were no delays. However, the sour face of the flight attendant at the gate entrance left no doubt that passengers were not being welcomed on board that day and that even the crew was anxious to cancel the flight.

As I settled onto the plane, I noticed as the last passengers were getting ready for departure and tightening their seat belts, that their facial expressions were grim—as if they expected this flight to be their last. The mood inside the airplane was an exact reflection of the gloomy weather outside.

Fifteen minutes later the Boeing 777 tilted its head toward the clouds and made a wide turn north, heading toward London. Climbing through the dark, the plane hit some thick clouds that made for a rather bumpy, unpleasant flight. The bumps that morning could have made even the strongest air passenger feel sick.

Twenty minutes after takeoff, something magical happened. The plane broke through the clouds into a crystal clear blue sky and the sun hit our eyes abruptly and unexpectedly. I looked at the view with astonishment. The grey clouds below looked strangely pretty in the strong sunlight.

However, the most amazing change that day occurred inside of the aircraft. The entire atmosphere began to change. The crew was smiling gracefully and chatting with passengers as they began serving breakfast. The passengers' faces suddenly brightened. People's attitudes began to change as well. They began to make pleasant conversations with one another, engaging each other in small talk. Everyone's spirits seem to have been magically lifted. The funny thing was that nothing had really changed. The weather was the same. It was still miserably cold and rainy in New Jersey. Only one thing had changed and that was…our point of view.

There is a great lesson to be learned from this situation.

In the gloomy, dark days of our life, when nothing seems to work out and the whole world seems to be against us, we need to take off and soar high above the clouds to find out that the sun is still there. Changing our point of view takes only a few seconds of halting our thoughts, igniting our imagination and flying high above the dark clouds that clutter our lives.

In doing so, we discover that the sun is still shining above the clouds even on the most gloomy of days. We will understand that the clouds that fog our life hide the happiness we could have enjoyed if we were only able to see it. We will realize that changing our perspective toward life also changes the reality of our life. We can still be happy during the unpleasant events that life brings from time to time; we just have to train ourselves to remember that the sun still shines above us—even if we can't see it right this moment.

Happiness shines through all of the time. We have to activate our mind to change our point of view in order to soar high above the clouds. This will allow us to eliminate the dark influence of the clouds so that we can enjoy enduring happiness. The next time your life and your day feel gloomy, think about flying high above the clouds and discovering that sunshine and happiness are still there and always will be.

BIBLIOGRAPHY

1. Robin Sharma, Leadership Wisdom from the Monk who sold his Ferrari, Hay House, 2009
2. Kevin Hogan, Talk Your Way to the Top, Advantage Quest Publications, 2007
3. Brian Tracy, How the Best Leaders Lead, AMACOM, 2010
4. Lawrence A. Bossidy, Ram Charan, Execution- The Discipline of Getting Things Done, Crown Business, 2002
5. Roger Connors, Tom Smith, How Did That Happen- Holding People Accountable for Results the Positive, Principled Way, 2009
6. Kevin and Jackie Freiberg, BOOM! 7 Choices For Blowing The Doors Off Business-As-Usual, Thomas Nelson Books, 2007
7. Seth Godin, Linchpin – Are You Indispensable? Portfolio, 2010
8. Emmanuel Gobillot, Leadershift – Reinventing Leadership for the Age of Mass Collaboration, Kogan Page, 2009
9. Jon R. Katzenbach and Zia Khan, Leading Outside the Liners - How to mobile the (in)formal Organization, Energize Your Team, and Get Better Results, Boos & Company, Inc.

10. James M. Kouzes and Barry Z. Posner, The Leadership Challenge, John Wiley and Sons Inc., 2007

11. Kerry Patterson, Joseph Grenny, Ron McMilan, and Al Switzler, Crucial Conversations – Tools for Talking When Stakes Are High, Mc Graw-Hill, 2002

12. Susan Scott, Fierce Conversations: Achieving Success at Work& in Life, One Conversation at a Time, The Berkley Publishing Group, 2002

13. Patrick M. Lencioni, The Five Temptations of a CEO: A Leadership Fable, Jossey-Bass, 1998

14. Patrick M. Lencioni, The Five Dysfunctions of a Team: A Leadership Fable, Jossey-Bass, 2002

15. John P. Kotter, What Leaders Really Do, Harvard Business Press, 1999

16. Ron Kaufman, Uplifting Service: The Proven Path to Delighting Your Customers, Colleagues, and Everyone Else You Meet, Evolve Publishing; 2012

ABOUT THE AUTHOR

Dave Osh has made it his life's mission to help corporate executives speed up their rise to the corner office and multiply their income—all while living healthy, fulfilling and love-filled lives.

Dave is the creator of the Corporate Entrepreneur Mastery program, author of the book Outgrow Middle Management - Accelerate Your Climb to the Top, the former CEO of a multinational corporation with revenues over $400M, with 500 employees and entities in 25 countries, the inventor of a patented product that was commercialized into a successful brand and the founder of an Internet enterprise,.

Dave's success can be seen not only through his own accomplishments, but also through the lives of his followers. He offers a proven blueprint for scaling the corporate pinnacle that has helped hundreds of people accelerate their career without scarifying their relationships, wellbeing and personal aspirations.

THREE FREE BONUS
TRAINING VIDEOS

"THE 6 SECRETS OF THE HIGHEST PAID EXECUTIVES"
By Dave Osh

Have you ever wondered how the most effective, highest paid, and super successful corporate executives achieve so much in their career and lives?

What they know, do, and focus on that enables them to earn millions of dollars in salaries and bonuses.

If you're stuck somewhere in in the middle, you will learn how to speed up your climb to the top of your organization, multiply your income, and accomplish your personal aspirations.

This special offer includes a personal live webinar with the author.

Access your bonus at http://goo.gl/NNN1c0.

You will then be prompted to enter your name and email address.

Printed in the USA
CPSIA information can be obtained
at www.ICGtesting.com
JSHW02233914082 4
68134JS00019B/1586